"Jonathan Edwards' *Religious A[* works of spiritual psychology pub Storms' unpacking of this significa 'Personal Narrative,' reveals once a so much deserves the most careful study today."
—MARK A. NOLL, Francis A. McAnaney Professor of History, University of Notre Dame

"Our churches desperately need spiritual discernment, and the *Affections* constitute perhaps the best manual on discernment ever written. But most Christians cannot wade through the immensity or prolixity of the original text. Therefore Storms' repackaging of this spiritual classic meets a serious need. Storms' essay on Edwards' personal spirituality, introducing the "Personal Narrative," is almost worth the price of the book. It is a marvelous synthesis and analysis. Then his running commentary, interspersed with direct selections from the Narrative, are exceedingly helpful."
—GERALD R. McDERMOTT, Professor of Religion, Roanoke College

"After nearly 300 years, these gems of Edwards continue to sparkle. It is no exaggeration to say that they stand as two of the best, most profound, and practically useful guides to everyday Christian living ever written. Sam Storms has done a superb job interpreting them for twenty-first century followers of Jesus. His vivid paraphrases are easy to read and always edifying. I pray that many will read and meditate upon this labor of love—and then move on to delve into Edwards' own writings."
—DOUGLAS A. SWEENEY, Trinity Evangelical Divinity School

"These texts of Jonathan Edwards have nourished the church for nearly three centuries, rightfully taking their place as classics. In Sam Storms' capable hands they'll now speak clearly, plainly, and powerfully to the church today and for generations to come. If you've ever wanted to tackle Edwards but have shied away, you no longer have an excuse."
—STEPHEN J. NICHOLS, author of *Heaven on Earth: Capturing Jonathan Edwards's Vision of Living in Between*

"In reading through this book, I feel like I am looking over Sam Storms' shoulder, reading Edwards together with him. At times, he pauses to interpret Edwards for me, at other times, he places Edwards' comments in their historical context. On rare occasions, he points out areas of disagreement, and at other times, he simply allows the profundity of Edwards' own words to speak for themselves. At all times, Sam's love and respect for Edwards shines through clearly."
—GLENN KREIDER, Professor of Theological Studies, Dallas Theological Seminary

SIGNS *of the* Spirit

SIGNS *of the*
Spirit

AN INTERPRETATION OF
Jonathan Edwards'
RELIGIOUS AFFECTIONS

SAM STORMS

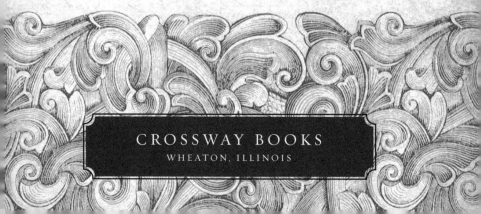

CROSSWAY BOOKS
WHEATON, ILLINOIS

Signs of the Spirit: An Interpretation of Jonathan Edwards'
"Religious Affections"

Copyright © 2007 by C. Samuel Storms

Published by Crossway Books
      a publishing ministry of Good News Publishers
      1300 Crescent Street
      Wheaton, Illinois 60187

Cover design: Jon McGrath

Cover illustration: iStock

First printing 2007

Printed in the United States of America

Scripture quotations occurring within direct quotations from Jonathan Edwards are from the King James Version of the Bible.

Unless marked KJV, all other Scripture quotations are from *The Holy Bible, English Standard Version®*, copyright © 2001 by Crossway Bibles, a publishing ministry of Good News Publishers. Used by permission. All rights reserved.

Library of Congress Cataloging-in-Publication Data
Storms, C. Samuel, 1951–
   Signs of the spirit : an interpretation of Jonathan Edwards'
"Religious affections" / Sam Storms.
      p. cm.
   Includes bibliographical references and index.
   ISBN 978-1-58134-932-0 (tpb)
   1. Edwards, Jonathan, 1703–1758. Treatise concerning the religious
affections. 2. Edwards, Jonathan, 1703–1758. Faithful narrative of the
surprising work of God. 3. Conversion—Christianity—History of
doctrines—18th century. 4. Emotions—Religious aspects—Christianity—
History of doctrines—18th century. I. Title.
BX7260.E3S76   2007
248.2—dc22   2007006232

VP		17	16	15	14	13	12	11	10	09	08	07
15	14	13	12	11	10	9	8	7	6	5	4	3	2	1

Affectionately dedicated to:

LYLE AND MARY DORSETT

Faithful friends, Lovers of God, Devoted to the Church
Ann and I will be forever grateful for your
sacrificial support, loving prayers, shepherd's heart,
and
godly example

CONTENTS

PART TWO
Personal Narrative

Preface

A BRIEF APOLOGETIC FOR
SIGNS OF THE SPIRIT

ASIDE FROM THE biblical authors themselves, no one has had greater influence on my life than Jonathan Edwards. I first became acquainted with him at the urging of Dr. John Hannah, longtime professor at Dallas Theological Seminary, from which I received my Th.M. in historical theology in 1973. John suggested that I undertake an independent studies course in Edwards and that I begin by reading his treatise on the *Freedom of the Will* (which eventually led to my writing a master's thesis on that volume). My first exposure to Edwards' *Religious Affections* came when John also insisted that it be included in the list of readings. I will forever be grateful for his wise counsel!

Because of the profound and truly life-changing influence that Edwards has exerted on me, I am quick to recommend his works to others, indeed, to everyone. This brings me to my defense of this interpretation of his treatise on the *Affections*. If people heeded my advice, I would hardly have undertaken this project. Nothing grieves me more than to hear that yet another has started reading Edwards only to give up, frustrated by his style or overwhelmed by the complexity of his argumentation.

I can't begin to count the number of times I've been asked for recommended reading and have suggested Edwards (specifically the *Religious Affections*), only to be greeted with a contorted face or an embarrassed evasion that goes something like this: "Well, I tried reading Edwards. I really wanted to read the *Affections*, but after about fifteen or twenty pages into it, I just quit. For whatever reason, I couldn't follow him. His style was aggravating and, well, to be honest, I just couldn't understand what he was saying."

Such confessions have come not only from average lay folk, but from well-educated seminary graduates as well. Edwards' penchant for torturously complex sentence structure, together with the abundance of theological "bunny trails" that, at least initially, don't seem to contribute to the point he is making, have tested and all too often triumphed over the determination of even the most avid and intellectual of Christians.

For years I have taken the high ground when it comes to the reading of Edwards, refusing to yield to the insistent demand that someone "tweak his prose" or paraphrase his theological concepts. I have faithfully exhorted countless men and women, again and again, to renew their commitment to working through some of Edwards' more daunting treatises. "Your patience and perseverance will reap a bountiful harvest," I have said again and again, to little (or no) avail I've come to discover. Sure, there are a few, here and there, who've made their way through the *Affections* and were (justifiably) proud of their journey. But even in the majority of these cases, they aren't sure they understood, far less appreciated and embraced, what they had read.

I've worked my way through the *Affections* at least ten times and I still struggle in places to make sense of Edwards. I'm more than happy to attribute this failure to my shortcomings rather than his (indeed, I still hesitate, at times, to acknowledge that he had *any* shortcomings!). But I can no longer escape the conclusion that no matter how passionately I exhort and encourage and rebuke and challenge people to read Edwards, no matter how exuberantly I promise them great treasure at the end of their labors, the vast majority of folk simply won't do it. Or they will read at most a few pages and then set aside the book, forever convinced that Edwards is beyond their grasp. I wish it were otherwise. I pray that it could be otherwise. But it isn't and, I fear, never will be.

The theology of Jonathan Edwards and his insight into the nature of religious experience are simply too important, too relevant, and too enriching to sacrifice on the altar of some lofty ideal that it is beneath his (and our) dignity to make his work accessible to a more general audience. I suppose I could go to my grave proudly congratulating myself for not having yielded to the temptation to do what this book proposes. But I'd go there with the disturbing realization that other people are likewise going there without having reaped the eternal benefits of what Edwards had to say. Let's be clear about something. I'm not advocating the "dumbing down" of Jonathan Edwards (or any aspect of the Christian faith). Yes, I would much prefer the "smarting up" of the Christian public, equipping them for the task of wrestling with this magnificent theological mind (and others as well). And I will continue to challenge believers of every age and educational background to think and dig deeply into the rich treasures of Christ, his Word, and the resources made available to his church throughout the last two millennia. My prayer is that *Signs of the Spirit* will be a helpful tool in the pursuit of that goal.

Nevertheless, I suspect that on reading this many will come to me, protesting, "Sam, you're wrong! I read the *Affections*. I loved it. Yes, it was really hard, but my perseverance paid off." Praise God for every one of them. But for every one of them there are one hundred others who tell a different story, whose encounter with Edwards was frustrating and embarrassing. It is for the latter that I wrote this book, not the former.

In my decision to write this book, I also had to overcome the comments of John E. Smith, who edited *Religious Affections* for the Yale University Press edition of Edwards' works (which is now at twenty-five volumes). In his editorial introduction, Smith wrote:

> In directing attention to his style, we cannot overlook the fact that many readers have found the *Affections* difficult going, nor should we ignore what is implied in the activity of the many editors who thought it necessary to rewrite the text. It is admittedly an exacting work; it calls for a reader's best effort. But there are rewards if we are willing to raise ourselves to the level of Edwards' austere standards; nothing is to be gained by bringing him down to a more facile plane in order to make him say what we would like to hear.[1]

"So, what say ye, Sam?" For the most part, I agree with Smith, at least with his conclusion that it is "difficult going," "an exacting work," shaped by "austere standards." But it would be a mistake to think that this book is an effort to bring him down to a "more facile

[1]John E. Smith, "Editor's Introduction," in Jonathan Edwards, *Religious Affections*, ed. John E. Smith, vol. 2 of The Works of Jonathan Edwards (New Haven, Conn.: Yale University Press, 1969), 8.

plane in order to make him say what we would like to hear." My goal
is to enable the reader to hear only what Edwards himself intended to
say. I'm simply attempting to bridge a rather cavernous gap between
how Edwards said it in the eighteenth century and how I believe he
would say it were he alive in the twenty-first century.

It would be easy to read Smith's words, nod our heads in agreement, and walk away with a smug complacency for having heeded his
warning. But that wouldn't result in more people reading Edwards! Or
at least not enough people would read him to justify that sort of well-
intentioned but idealistic response.

Many of you will contend that I've done a disservice to Edwards,
that I've failed to honor him for all that he has meant to me personally.
I hope that's not true. I would rather think that I've honored him in the
way he deserves by laboring to make accessible to as many people as
possible his marvelous insights into the Christian faith. So what exactly
have I done in this book? What is *Signs of the Spirit?*

As the subtitle indicates, this is an *interpretation* of the *Religious
Affections.* When it comes to Edwards' *Personal Narrative,* it is more
an *application,* but to include that in the subtitle would make it impos-
sibly cumbersome. So why do I call it an *interpretation?*

I had considered describing it as a *contemporary rendering,* but
that strikes me as a bit dishonest. The fact is, I *have* interpreted the
Religious Affections. To think otherwise would be both naïve and a
failure to recognize that I am rendering his work through my own theological and personal grid. Every time I choose to omit a particular paragraph, I am making an interpretive decision that inescapably reflects
what I regard as most important in the treatise. There are *reasons,* both
personal and philosophical, that govern my choices as to what is central and controlling in Edwards' work as over against what is secondary and peripheral. Every time I rewrite a paragraph or paraphrase an
argument or summarize a theological point, my own convictions are in
evidence. I think it's important that the reader understand this.

Of course, I wouldn't have undertaken this task if I didn't believe
that I truly understood what Edwards was getting at in his argument.
But I leave it to scholars more adept in Edwards than I to render a
judgment on my success. I'm certain that some readers who are familiar with Edwards will object to editorial decisions I've made as well as

theological interpretations that are reflected in my effort to make his lofty ideas not more "facile" but hopefully more intelligible. That's the risk one takes when writing a book like this. The strategy I followed is simple. I sat down over several months and read and reread the *Affections*, each time rewriting or articulating in a more understandable way the substance of Edwards' argument. I would determine, as best I could, what sections to omit, believing them to be tangential to the main argument or perhaps repetitive in a way that would only bog down the average reader (such as Edwards' many extended citations of supporting scriptural texts and extensive comments thereon). On many occasions, however, I have kept intact substantial portions of his work. These are indescribably rich and, yes, readable. There are, in fact, places where I quote Edwards at great length, with only an occasional attempt to interpret his comments. You should have no problem in recognizing the difference between Storms and Edwards, for direct citations together with an occasional colorful and vivid term of his are in quotation marks.

One more comment: I did not write this book so that people would read it *instead of* Edwards, but so that they might be motivated and better equipped to delve deeply into the original. Some may consider this rather idealistic, but surely it is no more so than disallowing a book such as this in the hopes that people will read the *Affections* in its entirety. In any case, I strongly encourage you to treat this volume as merely *preparatory* to your encounter with Edwards or perhaps as a *companion guide* to be read simultaneously with your reading of the original.

Grammatical and Stylistic Changes

Those who have read Edwards are familiar with his style (or, in some cases, the lack thereof!). He had a long-standing love affair with commas, splashing them pervasively throughout his writing. He used the colon and semicolon in ways that would be inadmissible in an English prose class today. He was no less infatuated with subordinate clauses, often constructing an elaborate sentence with as many as seven or eight of them. It's not unusual for him to say in five sentences what could as easily be said in one. On a number of occasions I have altered punctuation as well as reduced sentence length for the sake of readability. You will be the judge of whether I have succeeded.

Edwards also employed, as did virtually everyone in his day, certain abbreviations and grammatically incorrect words. For example, he typically uses "an" rather than "a" before a word beginning with "h." I've left these intact. I've also left unchanged his use of "'em" for "them," "'tis" for "it is," and "no" when we would expect "not."

Perhaps his most annoying habit is the use of "don't" when grammatical precision would call for "doesn't." However, I have chosen not to change these, for it would require a major reconstruction of the sentences in which they appear that would obscure rather than facilitate his meaning. Soon enough, as you read Edwards, you will become accustomed to this particular issue of his style.

There are also a few distinct words of which you need to be made aware. Edwards uses "wont" (don't mistake it for "won't") when he means something like "inclined" or "disposed to," and "actings" where we might prefer "actions." He will often use the word "discovery" when we would expect "revelation." Thus to have something "discovered" to you is to have it "revealed." Likewise, the plural "discoveries" is used instead of "revelations." As for spelling, I changed "Saviour" to "Savior" and "shew" to "show."

In only a few instances I have inserted a word, always bracketed, to fill out the flow of Edwards' argument. As noted, his excessive use of commas led me to eliminate many of them to conform to what most today are accustomed to reading. There are a number of places, on the other hand, where I inserted a comma in place of his use of a semicolon, or where I have replaced a colon with a period and then started a new sentence. Most of you, especially those unfamiliar with Edwards, won't even notice when this occurs.

I also made a decision, when quoting Edwards, not to include page numbers in the text from the many available versions of the *Affections* (all of which I used alternately, depending on which provided the more helpful rendering). See note 1 in the introduction to the *Affections* for a listing of them. I did this simply for ease of reading.

As for biblical texts cited, Edwards consistently used the King James Version, which I retained when citing him directly. In other instances the English Standard Version was used.

My treatment of his *Personal Narrative* followed many of the same principles, although I altered the original text of this short treatise only slightly. I did, however, eliminate certain portions that addressed issues of lesser importance. If you are wondering why I included the *Narrative* in a work that is primarily concerned with the *Religious Affections*, I encourage you to read the introduction to part two of this book. This, then, is my apologetic for *Signs of the Spirit*. Whether you agree with my editorial decisions or are offended by them, I hope you understand that I did it out of my immense respect for Edwards and my passion that his theological convictions be given a hearing in today's Christian world. We simply cannot afford to live in ignorance of the insights he brought to bear on the nature of spiritual experience. At least, I can't.

Sam Storms
October 2006

PART ONE

Religious Affections

Introduction

REVIVAL:
THE CONTEXT OF EDWARDS'
RELIGIOUS AFFECTIONS

JONATHAN EDWARDS' treatise *Religious Affections* is, in the opinion of many (myself included), the most important and accurate analysis of religious experience ever written. Edwards' primary concern in this work was to determine, as much as is possible, "what are the distinguishing qualifications of those that are in favor with God, and entitled to his eternal rewards."[1] Simply put, he endeavored to identify what constitutes true and authentic spirituality. Or, to put it in the form of a question: Are there certain features or characteristics in human thought and behavior that serve as "signs" of the saving activity and presence of the Spirit of God? Again, is it possible for us to know with any degree of certainty whether or not a person who claims to have experienced the saving grace of God is truly born again?

Edwards is famous for many things, among which was his habit of spending upwards of thirteen hours a day in his study. But it would be a mistake to think that he went about answering the question raised while sitting isolated in a theological ivory tower. Edwards' conclusions on this matter were forged in the fires of revival in eighteenth-century New England. Therefore, we can hardly afford to interpret this

---

[1] Jonathan Edwards, *Religious Affections*, ed. John E. Smith, vol. 2 of The Works of Jonathan Edwards (New Haven, Conn.: Yale University Press, 1969), 84. Edwards' treatise has been reproduced and printed in a number of forms, the two most helpful of which are the Yale University Press edition (which is based on the first edition published by S. Kneeland in Boston, 1746); and the Edward Hickman edition of *The Works of Jonathan Edwards*, 2 vols. (Carlisle, Pa.: Banner of Truth, 1979), 1:234–343 (found also in *The Religious Affections* [Carlisle, Pa.: Banner of Truth, 1991]), which is based on the Worcester edition of 1808. There is also available an abridged version, edited by James M. Houston, *Religious Affections: A Christian's Character Before God* (Minneapolis: Bethany, 1996). An online edition is also available at www.JonathanEdwards.com.

remarkable work apart from an understanding of the historical and religious context from which it emerged.

Great Awakenings

On May 30, 1735, Edwards wrote a letter of eight pages to Dr. Benjamin Colman (1673–1747), pastor of Brattle Street Church in Boston, in which he described the nature of the revival he was seeing. Colman forwarded a substantial portion of the letter to a friend in London, where news quickly spread about religious events in the Colonies. Edwards was in turn asked to write a more detailed account of what he had witnessed, which he titled, *A Faithful Narrative of the Surprising Work of God in the Conversion of many hundred souls in Northampton, and the Neighbouring Towns and Villages of the County of Hampshire, in the Province of the Massachusetts-Bay in New England.*[2]

Edwards completed work on the document on November 6, 1736. What he describes in this short book is the first wave of revival (1734–1736) that was later followed by what has come to be known as the Great Awakening (1740–1742).

Historical Precedents of the Revival

Revival was nothing new to the people of Massachusetts. Edwards was able to identify five so-called *harvests* under his predecessor and grandfather, Solomon Stoddard (who served as pastor in Northampton for sixty years). During each of these times of revival Edwards heard Stoddard say that "the greater part of the young people in the town, seemed to be mainly concerned for their eternal salvation."[3] The first wave of the Spirit's movement during Edwards' pastoral charge in Northampton may have initially been stirred by the unexpected deaths of two young people in a neighboring town, which "seemed to contribute to render solemn the spirits of many young persons; and there began evidently to appear more of a religious concern on people's minds."[4]

---

[2]The version of *A Faithful Narrative* cited here is found in *Jonathan Edwards on Revival* (Carlisle, Pa.: Banner of Truth, 1991), 2–74. It is also found, together with relevant correspondence, in the Yale edition of Edwards' works: Jonathan Edwards, "A Faithful Narrative," in *The Great Awakening,* ed. C. C. Goen, vol. 4 of The Works of Jonathan Edwards (New Haven, Conn.: Yale University Press, 1972), 99–211.
[3]Edwards, *Faithful Narrative,* 9.
[4]Ibid., 11.

Some scholars are inclined to dismiss any supernatural or divine cause for the revival and insist that it can be traced to the fearful reaction of the community to some natural calamity. Whereas it is true that a diphtheria epidemic struck New England from 1735 to 1740, Edwin Gaustad points out that

> the epidemic appeared in New Jersey in 1735, long after the revival movement had been under way there; in Connecticut and Massachusetts, the severity of the epidemic in any given area bears no observable relation to the intensity of the revival in that area, either before or after Whitefield; in New Hampshire the epidemic was all over by 1736, making difficult an explanation of the five-year lapse between its terminus and the beginning of the Great Awakening in the Kingston-Hampton Falls area; and finally, while the epidemic was from four to five times as severe in New Hampshire and Maine as in Connecticut and Massachusetts, it was in the latter area that the revival was most pervasive.[5]

Edwards himself connected the outbreak of spiritual renewal to a series of sermons he preached on justification by faith and the unusual conversion of an immoral young lady in the Northampton community (he discreetly referred to her as "one of the greatest company-keepers in the whole town"[6]).

Characteristics of the Revival

Without going into great detail, we should examine a few of the characteristic features of the awakening, as described by Edwards.

Edwards couldn't help but notice that the revival was, quite literally, the talk of the town: "Other discourse than of the things of religion," he noted, "would scarcely be tolerated in any company. The minds of people were wonderfully taken off from the world, it was treated amongst us as a thing of very little consequence."[7]

People were inclined to neglect their daily affairs, or at least subordinate them to the higher interest of the state of their souls. "They seemed to follow their worldly business, more as a part of their duty, than from any disposition they had to it; the tempta-

---

[5]Edwin S. Gaustad, *The Great Awakening in New England* (Gloucester, Mass.: Peter Smith, 1965), 20.
[6]Edwards, *Faithful Narrative*, 12.
[7]Ibid., 13.

tion now seemed to lie on that hand, to neglect worldly affairs too much, and to spend too much time in the immediate exercise of religion."[8] Their primary concern "was to get the kingdom of heaven, and every one appeared pressing into it. The engagedness of their hearts in this great concern could not *be hid*, it appeared in their very *countenances*."[9]

Edwards was especially impressed by the widespread impact of the awakening, citing more than thirty other communities where signs of renewal occurred. As for Northampton, "there was scarcely a single person in the town, old or young, left unconcerned about the great things of the eternal world."[10] There was also a remarkable transformation in the worship of God. "Our public praises," he observed, "were then greatly enlivened. . . . [People] were evidently wont to sing with unusual elevation of heart and voice, which made the duty pleasant indeed."[11] Above all else, the person of Jesus Christ became central in the thoughts and concerns of those involved.

Needless to say, the reaction of outside observers was mixed. "Many scoffed at and ridiculed it; and some compared what we called conversion, to certain distempers."[12] Others were so impressed that they spread word "that the state of the town could not be conceived of by those who had not seen it."[13] There were a number of instances, Edwards said, "of persons who came from abroad on visits, or on business, who had not been long here, before, to all appearances, they were savingly wrought upon, and partook of that shower of divine blessing which God rained down here, and went home rejoicing; till at length the same work began evidently to appear and prevail in several other towns in the county."[14]

Not only were the backslidden convicted and returned to the fold, many were saved. Edwards was confident "that more than 300 souls were savingly brought home to Christ, in this town [Northampton], in the space of half a year, and about the same number of males as females."[15]

---

[8]Ibid.
[9]Ibid.
[10]Ibid.
[11]Ibid., 14.
[12]Ibid., 15.
[13]Ibid.
[14]Ibid.
[15]Ibid., 19.

One of the more distinguishing features of the awakening was the acceleration or intensification of God's activity. Edwards described it this way: "God has also seemed to have gone out of his usual way, in the *quickness* of his work, and the swift progress his Spirit has made in his operations on the hearts of many. It is wonderful that persons should be so suddenly and yet so greatly changed."[16] Again, "when God in so remarkable a manner took the work into his own hands, there was as much done in a day or two, as at ordinary times, with all endeavours that men can use, and with such a blessing as we commonly have, is done in a year."[17]

The Nature of Conversions

Edwards was reluctant to suggest that true conversions followed a strict pattern or structure. Still, there appeared to be a consistency in that conversion generally entailed two stages.

First, there was typically a *deep and penetrating conviction of sin*. With some this occurred suddenly, whereas others experienced it gradually. The result was that they "quit their sinful practices; and the looser sort have been brought to forsake and dread their former vices and extravagances."[18] This was followed by their seeking the "means of salvation, reading, prayer, meditation, [and] the ordinances of God's house."[19] The "place of resort," Edwards wrote, "was now altered, it was no longer the tavern, but the minister's house that was thronged far more than ever the tavern had been wont to be."[20]

There was also variation in both the *degree* of fear experienced and the *duration* of it. There were a few instances in which individuals "had such a sense of God's wrath for sin . . . that they have been overborne; and made to cry out under an astonishing sense of their guilt, wondering that God suffers such guilty wretches to live upon earth, and that he doth not immediately send them to hell."[21]

The second dimension in the conversion experience was a *sense of God's love, mercy, and saving grace in Christ*. Again, Edwards explained:

---

[16]Ibid., 21.
[17]Ibid.
[18]Ibid., 23.
[19]Ibid., 24.
[20]Ibid.
[21]Ibid., 25–26.

It was very wonderful to see how person's affections were sometimes moved—when God did as it were suddenly open their eyes, and let into their minds a sense of the greatness of his grace, the fullness of Christ, and his readiness to save. . . . Their joyful surprise has caused their hearts as it were to leap, so that they have been ready to break forth into laughter, tears often at the same time issuing like a flood, and intermingling a loud weeping. Sometimes they have not been able to forbear crying out with a loud voice, expressing their great admiration.[22]

This overwhelming assurance of saving love had varied effects on the people:

Some persons having had such longing desires after Christ, or which have risen to such degree, as to take away their natural strength. Some have been so overcome with a sense of the dying love of Christ to such poor, wretched, and unworthy creatures, as to weaken the body. Several persons have had so great a sense of the glory of God, and excellency of Christ, that nature and life seemed almost to sink under it; and in all probability, if God had showed them a little more of himself, it would have dissolved their frame. . . . And they have talked, *when able to speak,* of the glory of God's perfections. . . .[23]

Many, while their minds have been filled with spiritual delights, have as it were forgot their food; their bodily appetite has failed, while their minds have been entertained *with meat to eat that others knew not of.*[24]

Edwards was duly impressed with the unparalleled joy of many, which often expressed itself in "earnest longings of soul to praise God."[25] Others expressed a new love for the Bible: "Some, by reason of their love to God's word, at times have been wonderfully delighted and affected at the sight of a Bible; and then, also, there was no time so prized as the Lord's day, and no place in this world so desired as God's house."[26]

Edwards observed, "Never, I believe, was so much done in confess-

[22]Ibid., 37–38.
[23]Ibid., 45.
[24]Ibid., 46.
[25]Ibid., 47.
[26]Ibid.

ing injuries, and making up differences, as the last year. Persons, after their own conversion, have commonly expressed an exceeding great desire for the conversion of others."[27] There was also a noticeable improvement in the physical condition of the community during the revival. "It was the most remarkable time of health that ever I knew since I have been in the town," Edwards observed. "We ordinarily have several bills put up, every sabbath, for sick persons; but now we had not so much as one for many sabbaths together. But after this [i.e., after the revival ended] it seemed to be otherwise."[28]

The End of the Revival

Although the history of revival reveals that no two outpourings were precisely the same, they do share one thing in common: they all came to an end. Edwards noted that "in the latter part of May, it began to be very sensible that the Spirit of God was gradually withdrawing from us, and after this time Satan seemed to be more let loose, and raged in a dreadful manner."[29] One event seemed to Edwards to hasten the demise of religion: a man, from a family prone to depression (what Edwards called "melancholy"), committed suicide by cutting his throat. "The devil took the advantage, and drove him into despairing thoughts."[30] [The man was in fact Joseph Hawley, Edwards' uncle.] The impact of this on the community was devastating:

> After this, multitudes in this and other towns seemed to have it strongly suggested to them, and pressed upon them, to do as this person had done. And many who seemed to be under no melancholy, some pious persons who had no special darkness or doubts about the goodness of their state . . . had it urged upon them as if somebody had spoke to them, *Cut your throat, now is a good opportunity. Now! Now!*[31]

The Spirit of God, "not long after this time, appeared very sensibly withdrawing from all parts of the country."[32] Nevertheless, Edwards was convinced that the vast majority of those who professed to having been saved in the revival "seem to have had an abiding change wrought

[27]Ibid.
[28]Ibid., 69.
[29]Ibid.
[30]Ibid., 70.
[31]Ibid.
[32]Ibid., 71.

on them; . . . they generally appear to be persons who have a new sense
of things, new apprehensions and views of God, of the divine attributes
of Jesus Christ, and the great things of the gospel."[33] Following the
revival of 1740–1742, with the benefit of hindsight, Edwards appeared
less confident.

The Revival of 1740–1742

The second wave of the Spirit's work, known to history as the First Great
Awakening, can generally be dated 1740–1742. Historians have typically
traced the revival's beginning to the visit of George Whitefield (1714–1771)
to America. Whitefield, "The Grand Itinerant," arrived in the fall of 1740
and "set all New England aflame with a revival compared to which the
Valley awakening of 1734–1735 was but a brush fire."[34]

After preaching to thousands all along the Atlantic coast, Whitefield
arrived in Edwards' Northampton in mid-October. After one Sunday
morning sermon in Edwards' church, Whitefield wrote in his diary
that "Good Mr. Edwards wept during the whole time of exercise.
The people were equally affected; and, in the afternoon, the power
increased yet more."[35]

Sarah Edwards was equally impressed. In a letter to her brother,
the Rev. James Pierpont of New Haven, she said:

> It is wonderful to see what a spell he casts over an audience by pro-
> claiming the simplest truths of the Bible. I have seen upward of a
> thousand people hang on his words with breathless silence, broken
> only by an occasional half-suppressed sob. He impresses the igno-
> rant, and not less the educated and refined . . . our mechanics shut up
> their shops, and the day-labourers throw down their tools to go and
> hear him preach, and few return unaffected. . . . Many, very many
> persons in Northampton date the beginning of new thoughts, new
> desires, new purposes and a new life, from the day they heard him
> preach of Christ.[36]

Benjamin Franklin, although an unbeliever, regarded Whitefield to
be his friend and said this of his oratorical gift:

[33]Ibid.
[34]Goen, "Editor's Introduction," in Edwards, Great Awakening, 48.
[35]Ibid., 49.
[36]Cited in Arnold A. Dallimore, George Whitefield: God's Anointed Servant in the Great Revival of
the Eighteenth Century (Westchester, Ill.: Crossway, 1990), 89–90.

He had a loud and clear voice, and articulated his words so perfectly
that he might be heard and understood at a great distance, especially
as his auditories observed the most perfect silence. . . . By hearing him
often, I came to distinguish easily between sermons newly composed
and those which he had often preached in the course of his travels.
His delivery of the latter was so improved by frequent repetition, that
every accent, every emphasis, every modulation of the voice, was so
perfectly well turned and well placed, that, without being interested in
the subject, one could not help being pleased with the discourse.[37]

According to C. C. Goen, "By the time he passed from Connecticut
into New York, his journal showed that he had spent 45 days, visited
40 towns, and delivered 97 sermons and exhortations."[38] Whitefield
set sail for England on January 16, 1741, after fourteen and a half
months of preaching in America. He returned for a brief visit in the
fall of 1744.

Whitefield was far from the only participant in this awakening.
One must also mention Gilbert Tennent (1703–1764), leader of the
Presbyterian revival in the middle Colonies. Goen reports that "after
Tennent passed through eastern Connecticut, emotional outbursts in
time of worship became common. Preachers sometimes had to stop in
mid-sermon, as 'weeping, sighs and sobs' mingled with cries of distress:
'Alas! I'm undone; I'm undone! O, my sins! How they prey upon my
vitals! What will become of me? How shall I escape the damnation of
hell, who have spent away a golden opportunity under Gospel light, in
vanity?'"[39] Visions and trances, evidently, were commonplace. Chief
among Tennent's messages was his belief that most ministers of the
day were unconverted. Needless to say, this didn't fare well with the
established clergy of New England!

Yet another preacher, of a decidedly different disposition, was
James Davenport (1716–1757). Davenport was labeled an "enthusiast" and was in many ways responsible for those excesses that Edwards
believed led to the end of the revival. "Enthusiasm," as Goen defines it,
"is belief in God's immediate inspiration or possession, leading often
to claims of divine authority."[40]

[37]Cited in Gaustad, *Great Awakening in New England*, 29.
[38]Goen, "Editor's Introduction," in Edwards, *Great Awakening*, 49.
[39]Ibid., 51.
[40]Ibid., 62.

Charles Chauncy, principal opponent of the revival (see below), applied the word to Davenport "in a bad sense, as intending an imaginary, not a real inspiration: according to which sense, the Enthusiast is one who has a conceit of himself as a person favored with the extraordinary presence of the Deity. He mistakes the workings of his own passions for divine communications, and fancies himself immediately inspired by the Spirit of God, when all the while he is under no other influence than that of an overheated imagination."[41]

Opposition and Division

Opposition to the awakening was fierce and persistent. Charles Chauncy (1705–1787), pastor of Boston's most influential church, led the opposition. Chauncy was the acknowledged leader of the "Old Lights," those who "vilified the whole revival as 'the effect of enthusiastic heat.'"[42] Chauncy and his supporters typically preferred the time-honored traditions of the established order of religion in New England and opposed the new measures introduced by the revivalists. For them, conversion was principally a transformation in one's intellectual convictions. The Christian life, therefore, together with any alleged encounter with the Spirit, must be reasonable, courteous, and not given to visible or vocal displays of emotion.

Chauncy's principal objections to the revival were published in September 1743, in a work entitled *Seasonable Thoughts on the State of Religion in New England* (Boston, 1743). Among other concerns, he cited the ill effects of itinerant ministry, especially among those not ordained to the task of preaching. "Besides creating jealousies and threatening prerogatives," said Chauncy, "itineracy flaunted the Congregational theory of the ministerial office."[43]

He also objected to "lay exhorters." One critic wrote, "There is a creature here whom perhaps you never heard of before. It is called an Exhorter. It is of both sexes, but generally of the male, and young. Its distinguished qualities are ignorance, impudence, zeal. Numbers of these Exhorters are amongst the people here. They go from town to town, creep into houses, lead captive silly women, and then the men.

---

[41]Ibid.
[42]Ibid., 63.
[43]Cited in Gaustad, *Great Awakening in New England,* 70.

Such of them as have good voices do great execution as they mov
hearers, make them cry, faint, swoon, fall into convulsions."[44]
Chauncy was especially offended by what he perceived to be
fanatical excess in the behavior of those who participated in the revival.
True religion, Chauncy said, was primarily a matter of the mind, not
the affections, and was characterized by self-control, cultural sophisti-
cation, and strict moral propriety. "The plain truth is [that] an *enlightened mind,* and not *raised affections,* ought always to be the guide
of those who call themselves men; and this, in the affairs of religion,
as well as other things."[45] One should not conclude from this that
Edwards denigrated the mind, as will become evident in the subsequent
analysis of his treatise. George Marsden is quick to point out that "as
any perusal of Edwards' sermons will confirm, Edwards' exaltation of
the affections was never at the expense of reason."[46]

By the end of 1743, Gaustad observes, "all the principles, even
most of the details, of criticism of the revival had been established.
The Great Awakening was dead, although many were trying to force
air into its lungs while others were still hacking at the corpse whenever
possible." [47]

Numerous explanations for the diminishing influence of the revival
have been suggested, and Edwards had his own opinion. But Gaustad
looks at what happened with the common sense of a historian:

> From our vantage point, no special perspicacity is required to
> conclude that the religious intensity of 1741 could not long be
> maintained. The dreadful concerns, the traumatic awakenings, the
> accelerated devotion—these by their nature are of limited duration.
> The fever pitch must soon pass, else the patient dies. . . . The ebb
> of this flood of revivalism would seem then to require no elaborate
> explanation: it declined simply because it had to, because society
> could not maintain itself in so great a disequilibrium.[48]

Gaustad may be right, but one cannot ignore the devastating effects of
unbridled fanaticism and emotionalism (see below).

---

[44]Ibid., 72.
[45]Cited in George M. Marsden, *Jonathan Edwards: A Life* (New Haven, Conn.: Yale University
Press, 2003), 281.
[46]Ibid., 282.
[47]Gaustad, *Great Awakening in New England,* 79.
[48]Ibid., 61–62.

Edwards' Defense of the Awakening

Throughout the revivals and well into their aftermath, Edwards consistently defended the work as being, in general, of divine origin. He disapproved of "enthusiasm," subjectivism, and those excesses which Davenport insisted were sure signs of the Spirit's work, but did not believe these peripheral problems invalidated the legitimacy of what God was doing.

In hopes of putting an end to what they deemed extravagant and "enthusiastic" behavior on the part of a number of students, the administration at Yale invited Edwards to deliver the commencement speech on September 10, 1741. What they heard instead was a spirited defense, in general, of the spiritual authenticity of the revival.

Edwards later expanded on the work and published it that same year with a preface by the Rev. William Cooper of Boston. The complete title is:

> The Distinguishing Marks of a Work of the Spirit of God, Applied to that Uncommon Operation that has lately Appeared on the Minds of Many of the People of This Land: With a Particular Consideration of the Extraordinary Circumstances with Which this Work Is Attended.[49]

Edwards' design was "to show what are the true, certain, and distinguishing evidences of a work of the Spirit of God, by which we may safely proceed in judging of any operation we find in ourselves, or see in others."[50]

His approach was twofold. He began with what we might call "Negative Signs," or events, experiences, and religious phenomena from which we may conclude *nothing*. One is not free to deduce from the presence of these occurrences either that the Holy Spirit produced them or that he did not. They may well be the fruit of the Spirit's activity, but then again they may just as easily be the result of human weakness or emotional instability or the product of a manipulative evangelist. Scripture simply doesn't provide explicit guidelines by which we may know.

---

[49]The version of *Distinguishing Marks* used here is found in *Jonathan Edwards on Revival*, 75–147. See also Edwards, "The Distinguishing Marks," in Goen, ed., *Great Awakening*, 213–288.
[50]Edwards, *Distinguishing Marks*, 87.

Edwards then turned to those signs which are sure and certain evidence of the Spirit's work. He proceeds "to show positively what are the sure, distinguishing Scripture evidences and marks of a work of the Spirit of God, by which we may proceed in judging of any operation we find in ourselves, or see among a people without danger of being misled."[51] Here Edwards based his argument on principles gleaned from 1 John 4:1–6.

Responding to the Revival

The revivals surfaced an acute problem, with both theological and pastoral implications, that ultimately accounts for Edwards' writing of the *Religious Affections*. The problem is actually twofold. First, what is the nature of true religion? What constitutes the essence of that life which is pleasing and acceptable to God? Second, are there criteria by which we can differentiate between true and false religion, between the holy and the hypocrite, between authentic and spurious piety? How does one determine, if at all, who has been the object of the Spirit's saving work? Can we, with any degree of confidence, distinguish between the gracious presence of the Spirit on the one hand, and his more common, non-salvific, activity on the other?

Edwards' answer to the first question, contra Chauncy, is that "true religion, in great part, consists in holy affections."[52] His answer to the second question comes in the form of twenty-four "signs" by which we may discern the difference between true and false spirituality. There are twelve signs that prove nothing either way. They neither demonstrate that one *has* been a recipient of the Spirit's saving work nor that one *has not*. They are experiences that could as easily come from the flesh as from the Spirit. They require no supernatural or divine source to account for their presence and are thus a poor standard by which to judge the state of one's soul.

There are twelve additional signs, however, that point us to the presence of saving grace and the essence of what it is to be a child of God. As John E. Smith has pointed out, not only are these twelve signs "tests or standards of genuine piety, but they are themselves the very substance of the religious life."[53]

---

[51]Ibid., 109.
[52]Edwards, *Religious Affections*, 95.
[53]Smith, "Editor's Introduction," in Edwards, *Religious Affections*, 11.

Again, "Edwards never lost sight of the twofold task that followed: on the one hand, to defend the central importance of the affections against those who would eliminate them from religion; and on the other, to provide criteria for testing them lest religion degenerate into emotional fanaticism and false enthusiasm."[54] Thus Edwards' treatise "brings together two lines of thought: it identifies the activity of the Holy Spirit with the affections in the soul and at the same time shows how these same affections when properly tested enable us to discriminate genuine from false piety."[55]

Many, such as Davenport and his followers, claimed that they were recipients of the Spirit's grace because they experienced a wide range of physical phenomena, whether shaking or shouting, laughing or weeping, or other overt displays of what they considered genuine religious zeal. Edwards himself was witness to folk who "lost their bodily strength" (i.e., fell to the ground), including his own wife, Sarah. Others testified to seeing visions, hearing voices, or otherwise feeling "impressions" on the "imagination." At times, some would fall into a trance-like state and would remain therein for twenty-four hours or longer.

Were such physical manifestations and convulsions a sure sign of the Spirit's work? Or were they in every instance the product of manipulative ministers who excelled in unleashing the emotions of unsuspecting sheep? Neither, said Edwards. Such physical phenomena *may* be the result of the Spirit's encounter with the frailty of human nature. But maybe *not*. In any case they are insufficient grounds on which to base one's assurance of salvation and by no means constitute the essence of the religious life.

As we work our way through the *Affections* we must keep in mind that Edwards will argue, against Chauncy, that true religion consists not merely of a "notional" understanding and cognitive acquiescence to truth, but of a "sense of the heart" in which lively and vigorous affections of love and delight and joy and peace and yearning are in evidence. Such affections, said Edwards, *may* be accompanied by physiological phenomena, but the presence of the latter was no sure proof of the reality of the former. We must also remember that Edwards will argue, against Davenport, that physiological phenomena, in and

---

[54]Ibid., 17.
[55]Ibid.

of themselves, prove nothing about the reality of spiritual experience. We should not be surprised, Edwards said, if the body reacts in strange and manifest ways to what the mind perceives, but bodily actions can as easily be the result of any number of purely natural (not to mention demonic), physiological, and psychological factors that have nothing to do with the special saving grace of the Holy Spirit.

Yet, in spite of the undeniable excesses and emotional extremes to which Davenport and others took the revival, Edwards saw in the midst of it a genuine work of God. He was not in the least inclined to throw out what he regarded as a live baby simply because some had dirtied the bathwater with the soil of their religious delusions.

With hindsight Edwards acknowledged that he had been somewhat naïve in his belief that as many had been saved as had claimed to be. In the aftermath of revival he had witnessed and worked with far too many folk who quickly fell away from their initial zeal and profession of faith. Without dismissing the revival altogether, he became ever more convinced that the subjective experiences and physical manifestations on which many based their assurance of salvation were a poor and misleading foundation on which to build. As Michael Haykin has pointed out, "Much of the problem lay in the fact that many of the congregation had wrong notions about the way of ascertaining a genuine conversion. Too much weight was placed upon 'impressions on the imagination' and specific experiences, and not enough consideration given to what Edwards calls 'the abiding sense and temper of their hearts' and 'fruits of grace.'"[56]

What, then, is the nature of a genuine and saving encounter with the Spirit of God? What are the criteria by which we might determine if we have been the recipients of his redemptive grace? This was the question to which Edwards applied himself in his treatise on the *Religious Affections*.[57]

---

[56]Michael A. G. Haykin, *Jonathan Edwards: The Holy Spirit in Revival* (Webster, N.Y.: Evangelical Press, 2005), 48.

[57]Although there have been countless articles in scholarly journals analyzing the *Affections*, there have been few attempts to explain this remarkable work for a more popular audience. The best, in my opinion, is still that of Gerald R. McDermott, *Seeing God: Twelve Reliable Signs of True Spirituality* (Downers Grove, Ill.: InterVarsity, 1995). It has been released in a second edition by Regent College Publishing under the title *Seeing God: Jonathan Edwards and Spiritual Discernment* (2000).

1

THE ESSENCE OF TRUE SPIRITUALITY

I DOUBT IF THERE IS a more pressing and urgent issue for the church today than determining "what are the distinguishing qualifications of those that are in favor with God, and entitled to his eternal rewards." Or to put it in other words, what is the nature of true spirituality and those features in the human soul that are acceptable in the sight of God?

To answer this question we turn our focus to 1 Peter 1:8. There the apostle described his Christian audience in these encouraging terms: "Though you have not seen him, you love him. Though you do not now see him, you believe in him and rejoice with joy that is inexpressible and filled with glory." Why this passage? Why should we believe it describes the quintessence of true spirituality more than any other?

The answer is found in the immediately preceding context (vv. 6–7), in which Peter describes the trials and suffering of the believer. Such experiences have a unique capacity to highlight the differences between what is true and sincere in the heart of a person as over against what is false and hypocritical. Hardship in its many forms and the testing of our faith cause the "genuine beauty and amiableness" of true spirituality to appear more clearly. Indeed, "true virtue never appears so lovely, as when it is most oppressed."

Perhaps most important of all is that trials and pains purify and increase true spirituality. They not only enable us to see and discern what is true from what is false, but also "tend to refine it, and deliver it from those mixtures of that which is false, which encumber and impede it, [so] that nothing may be left but that which is true." From the comparison Peter draws in verse 7, we see that "as gold that is tried in the fire, is purged from its alloy and all remainders of dross, and comes forth more solid and beautiful; so true faith being tried as gold is tried in the fire, becomes more precious; and thus also is found unto praise, and honor, and glory."

As noted, the apostle is writing to Christians who are enduring excruciating persecution, oppression, and affliction. One need only read 1 Peter 1:6; 2:20–21; 3:17; and especially 4:12–18 to see that this is true. He makes it clear in chapter 1 that our ability to rejoice simultaneously with the anguish of trials and troubles is based on two things.

Peter first reminds his readers of the *duration* of trials and suffering. He says in verse 6 that they are "for a little while." In other words, they are temporary, not eternal. Trials and pain will pass. No matter how bad it gets here on earth, one day our suffering will give way to the unsurpassed glory and eternal pleasure of heaven (see 2 Cor. 4:16–18). Knowing the duration of trials and suffering gives us strength to persevere and endure.

Second, he points to the *design* of trials. In verse 7 Peter says that suffering works to purify our faith. His point is that God never wastes pain. The trials and tribulations of this life serve to sanctify us and conform us to the image of Jesus himself. First Peter 1:7 thus reminds us of two verses in Psalm 119:

> Before I was afflicted I went astray,
>   but now I keep your word (119:67).

> It is good for me that I was afflicted,
>   that I may learn your statutes (119:71).

Peter's point is that just as fire burns away the dross and alloy from gold, leaving it pure and solid, so also the flames of trials and tests and oppression consume the dross of our faith. When we are subjected to the heat of persecution and tribulation, hypocrisy, pride, and self-sufficiency are progressively (though never perfectly) destroyed (see Ps. 66:10; Mal. 3:3; Isa. 48:10).

When we come to verse 8 we find Peter describing for us what remains of Christian faith that has passed through the furnace of afflictions. In other words, verse 8 describes the end product of persecution and pain. It describes Christian faith in its rawest and purest form, the most holy essence of faith. This is "grade-A" faith, faith that is as free as it can be, this side of heaven, of sinful additives and preservatives! Here is faith as it has never been seen before. Here is faith with the peripheral elements pared off, its spurious and superficial and hypocritical dregs drained away. In sum, verse 8 describes the very essence of authentic Christianity.

Let me illustrate what Peter means. Try to envision a solid block of granite, untouched by human hands. When a master sculptor approaches such an object, he takes hammer and chisel and, in effect, begins to chip away everything that doesn't look like a man! He cuts, shapes, and pounds away until the finished product stands before us in all its glory. That's what God does with us through our trials and oppressive circumstances. God uses them like a spiritual hammer and chisel to chip away from our lives everything that doesn't look like Jesus! He pares away every false prop, every transient hope. The result is what Peter describes in 1 Peter 1:8.

Or consider the athlete who fails to work out. He becomes slothful, eating and drinking and refusing to exercise. Over time his muscles atrophy. He gains excessive weight. His reflexes aren't as sharp as they used to be. His lung capacity is greatly reduced. When he runs (if he ever gets off the couch), his legs feel heavy and lifeless. Then he recommits himself to a rigorous exercise program. Over the next few weeks he burns away body fat and strengthens his muscles. His endurance level increases, and he returns to his former shape. The result is a finely honed body, ready for competition. The physical effect of exercise on his body is analogous to the spiritual effect of trials on our faith.

So what am I saying? Simply this: 1 Peter 1:8 portrays for us what Christian faith looks like in its purest form. Here is *true* spirituality, *authentic* religion, seen as clearly and as transparently this side of final glorification as is possible.

And of what does true spirituality consist? Peter identifies two things: *love for Jesus* and *joy in Jesus*. Though his readers did not see Christ with the physical eye, their spiritual vision was one of unashamed and extravagant affection for the Son of God. Though their outward suffering was grievous and painful, their inner joy was a pleasure of such depth that no trial could diminish it.

There are two things Peter says of this joy. The first is the manner or means by which it rises in the human heart, namely, through faith, belief, and trust in the Son of God. Peter appears to say that it is *because* you believe in him that such joy fills the heart. But second, this is no ordinary joy, no fleeting happiness, no passing pleasure. It is "inexpressible" joy that is "filled with glory" (v. 8). This joy is "of a vastly more pure, sublime and heavenly nature" than worldly joy, "being something supernatural, and truly divine, and so ineffably excellent; the sublimity, and exquisite sweetness of which, there were no words to set forth." This is a joy that is so profound that it is beyond words. It is all-consuming, overwhelming, speechless joy! This joy defies all human efforts at understanding or explanation. The words have not yet been created that would do justice to the depths of this kind of joy. The human tongue has not yet been found that can articulate the heights to which this kind of joy elevates us.

This joy is also "filled with glory"; it is "glorified joy"! "In rejoicing with this joy, their minds were filled, as it were, with a glorious brightness, and their natures exalted and perfected. It was a most worthy, noble rejoicing that did not corrupt and debase the mind, as many carnal joys do, but did greatly beautify and dignify it. It was a prelibation of the joy of heaven that raised their minds to a degree of heavenly blessedness."

The word Peter employs evokes images of God's glory in the Old Testament, that bright, shining radiance of his presence. This, then, is a joy shot through and through with the resplendent majesty of the beauty of God's being. It is not fleshly or worldly joy, nor the joy that comes from earthly achievements or money or fame. It is a joy that has been baptized, as it were, in the glory of God himself.

From Peter's incredible utterance, we may draw the conclusion that true spirituality or true religion consists in great measure in *holy affections*. Or again, "when religion appeared in them most in its genuine excellency and native beauty, and was found to praise, and honor, and glory, [Peter] singles out the religious affections of love and joy, that were then in exercise in them. These are the exercises of religion he takes notice of, wherein their religion did thus appear true and pure and in its proper glory."

But we must define the word "affection." What does it mean? How does it differ, if at all, from our word "emotion"? Is it the same as the word "passion"? And does Peter really believe true spirituality to consist in holy affections? And are there other affections aside from love and joy that Scripture identifies as embodying the essence of authentic faith? These are the questions we will take up in the next chapter.

2

SPIRITUAL AFFECTIONS

THE WORD "AFFECTION" may be unfamiliar to many, except when used of romantic feelings between a man and a woman. This is not the sense in which I use it here. The affections are simply "the more vigorous and sensible exercises of the inclination and will of the soul." To make sense of this we must first account for the way God has constituted the human soul.

God has created the soul with two faculties: "one is that by which it is capable of perception and speculation, or by which it discerns and views and judges of things; which is called the understanding." Most would simply use the word "mind" to describe this faculty.

The other faculty is that by which the soul goes beyond mere perception or understanding and is in some way either inclined toward or averse to what it grasps. In other words, the soul is not an indifferent or unaffected spectator but either likes or dislikes, is pleased or displeased, approves or rejects what it sees. Some call this faculty the *inclination*. When we have in view those actions that are governed by it we refer to it as the *will*. Perhaps its most common designation is the *heart*.

Whatever the mind or understanding perceives, the inclination either is pleased with and approves of or opposes and disapproves of. Certainly there are varying degrees of both delight and disgust. Some ideas or objects elicit intense disdain, while others stir deep and heartfelt joy. Still other things that our minds grasp have comparatively little impact on us. Although we are rarely utterly indifferent to them, our souls are not greatly stirred.

On the other hand, when we see, perceive, think about, or ponder things or ideas that greatly engage us, even our bodies are powerfully affected. God has so united the material (body) and immaterial (soul) aspects of our being that it is virtually impossible for the latter to be greatly moved and it not affect the former. The word "affections," therefore, describes the more "vigorous and sensible exercises" of this faculty of soul by which we are either greatly drawn to or driven from some reality as perceived by the understanding. Affections, then, are warm and fervid inclinations that reveal the fundamental orientation of the human heart.

In the course of human existence, we make countless choices; we exercise our wills in the pursuit of some option to the exclusion of another. But only those acts of will that are lively and sensible and vigorous deserve the name *affections*.

Every time we exercise our will, we give evidence of either liking or disliking what is in view. We are either inclined or disinclined toward some object or course of action. If our inclination toward something "be in a high degree, and be vigorous and lively, [it] is the very same thing with the affection of love [or desire, joy, delight]; and that disliking and disinclining, if in a great degree, is the very same with hatred."

Such lively and sensible and vigorous affections of the soul invariably have an effect on the body in some way and to varying degrees. Indeed, "such seems to be our nature and such the laws of the union of soul and body, that there never is any case whatsoever [of] any lively and vigorous exercise of the will or inclination of the soul without some effect upon the body, in some alteration of the motion of its fluids, and especially of the animal spirits. And on the other hand, from the same laws of the union of soul and body, the constitution of the body, and the motion of its fluids, may promote the exercise of the affections."

It's important to remember, however, that the mind, not the body, is the seat and source of spiritual affections. Only the soul or immaterial element is capable of thinking and understanding, and thus of loving or hating, or experiencing joy or sorrow over what is known. The many physiological sensations we experience—the rush of blood, rapid breathing, goose bumps, chills down the spine, an increased heartbeat, etc.—are but effects of affections and are not to be identified with them. Thus a disembodied spirit "may be as capable of love and hatred, joy or sorrow, hope or fear, or other affections, as one that is united to a body." The saints now with Christ in heaven, as also the angels and even God himself, are filled with holy and intense spiritual affections, yet they do not have a physical body or blood or adrenaline or hormones or literal eyes, ears, and noses.

So how do "affections" differ from "passions"? Perhaps the latter refer to those inclinations of the will that "are more sudden, and whose effects on the animal spirits are more violent, and the mind more overpowered, and less in its own command."

We should also distinguish affections from "emotions" or "feelings." Certainly there is what may rightly be called an emotional dimension to affections. Affections, after all, are sensible and intense longings or aversions of the will. Perhaps it would be best to say that whereas affections are not less than emotions, they are surely more. Emotions can often be no more than physiologically heightened states of either euphoria or fear that are unrelated to what the mind perceives as true. Affections, on the other hand, are *always* the fruit or effect of what the mind understands and knows. The will or inclination is moved either toward or away from something that is perceived by the mind. An emotion or mere feeling, on the other hand, can rise or fall independently of and unrelated to anything in the mind.

One can experience an emotion or feeling without it properly being an affection, but one can rarely if ever experience an affection without it being emotional and involving intense feelings that awaken and move and stir the body.

True spirituality, or true religion, therefore, consists to a large extent in "vigorous and lively actings of the inclination and will of the soul, or the fervent exercises of the heart," which is to say, the affections.

Our next task will be to demonstrate from the biblical text itself that this proposition is true.

3

BIBLICAL FOUNDATIONS FOR UNDERSTANDING THE AFFECTIONS

THE SORT OF RELIGION or spirituality that pleases God is one that consists largely in "vigorous and lively actings of the inclination and will of the soul, or the fervent exercises of the heart." God is displeased with weak, dull, and lifeless inclinations. Scripture speaks often and with divine approval of earnest and fervent affections of the soul (see Rom. 12:11; Deut. 10:12; 6:4–5; 30:6).

Spirituality is actually of little benefit to anyone if not characterized by lively and powerful affections. Nothing is so antithetical to true religion as lukewarmness. Consider those many biblical texts in which our relationship to God is compared to "running, wrestling or agonizing for a great prize or crown, and fighting with strong enemies that seek our lives, and warring as those that by violence take a city or kingdom."

Whereas it is true that new Christians will have affections that are comparatively weak, "yet everyone that has the power of godliness in his heart has his inclinations and heart exercised towards God and divine things, with such strength and vigor, that these holy exercises do prevail in him above all carnal or natural affections, and are effectual to overcome them."

Not only are affections the essence of true spirituality, they are also the spring or source of virtually all our actions. There is hardly any activity or pursuit of man that is not, to some degree, driven or influ-

enced by love, hatred, desire, hope, fear, etc. If we were to eliminate
from the world all love, hatred, hope, fear, anger, zeal, and desire, that
is to say, all affections of the soul, the world would lie motionless and
dead. Whether it be covetousness or greed or ambition or sensuality or
any such worldly experience, apart from such affections energizing this
activity mankind would be passive and uninvolved.

Consider for a moment why so many hear the Word of God and
respond so pathetically. They hear of the glorious perfections of God,
his almighty power and boundless wisdom, his majesty and holiness,
his goodness and mercy; they hear of the unspeakable love of God and
of the great things that Christ has done and suffered; they hear of the
beauty of heaven and the misery of hell, and yet they "remain as they
were before, with no sensible alteration on them, either in heart or
practice, because they are not affected with what they hear; and ever
will be so till they are affected. I am bold to assert, that there never was
any considerable change wrought in the mind or conversation of any
one person, by anything of a religious nature, that ever he read, heard
or saw, [who] had not his affections moved." In other words, it is only
as people are affected by the great truths of Christianity that they are
moved to love God and seek him and plead with him in prayer and be
brought low in humility and repentance. Simply put, affections are the
spring and source of virtually all significant spiritual endeavors.

A close look at Scripture will reveal that true spirituality consists
in a variety of affections. For example, there is godly fear, consisting
in a trembling at God's Word, as well as hope (see Jer. 17:7; Ps. 31:24;
33:18; 146:5; 147:11; Rom. 8:24; 1 Thess. 5:8; Heb. 6:19; 1 Pet. 1:3)
and hatred (see Prov. 8:13; Ps. 97:10; 101:2–3; 119:104; 139:21).
Many times we read of holy desire, expressed in longings, hungering
and thirsting after God and holiness (see Isa. 26:8; Ps. 27:4; 42:1–2;
63:1–2; 84:1–2). We are often commanded to experience joy (see Ps.
37:4; 97:12; 33:1; 149:2; Matt. 5:12; Phil. 3:1; 4:4; 1 Thess. 5:16).
Similarly, sorrow, mourning, and brokenness of heart, all of which are
deep and moving affections of the soul, are portrayed as essential to
true spirituality (see Matt. 5:4; Ps. 34:18; 51:17; Isa. 57:15; 61:1–2;
66:2). In addition, there is gratitude, compassion and mercy (see Isa.
57:1; Ps. 37:21; Prov. 14:31; Col. 3:12; Matt. 5:7; 23:23; Mic. 6:8;
Hos. 6:6), and zeal (see Titus 2:14; Rev. 3:15–19).

Perhaps nothing is mentioned so frequently as the holy affection of love (among the multitude of texts, consider Matt. 22:37–40; Rom. 13:8; Gal. 5:14; 1 Tim. 1:5; 1 Cor. 13). "Now although it be true, that the love thus spoken of, includes the whole of a sincerely benevolent propensity of the soul, towards God and man; yet it may be considered, that it is evident from what has been before observed, that this propensity or inclination of the soul, when in sensible and vigorous exercise, becomes *affection,* and is no other than affectionate love. And surely it is such vigorous and fervent love which Christ speaks of, as the sum of all religion, when he speaks of loving God with all our hearts, with all our souls, and with all our minds, and our neighbor as ourselves, as the sum of all that was taught and prescribed in the law and the prophets."

But love is not simply one of many affections: it is the first and chief and fountain of all the affections. "From love arises hatred of those things which are contrary to what we love, or which oppose and thwart us in those things that we delight in. It is from the various exercises of love and hatred, according to the circumstances of the objects of these affections, as present or absent, certain or uncertain, probable or improbable, that arise all those other affections of desire, hope, fear, joy, grief, gratitude, anger, etc."

Out of vigorous, fervent, affectionate love for God arise an intense hatred and abhorrence of sin, a dread of God's displeasure, gratitude for his goodness, delight in God when we sense his gracious presence, and grief when he seems distant.

Examples from the Lives of the Saints

We can see that true spirituality consists largely in holy affections by noting several of the more prominent saints in Scripture. We see the centrality of affections in David's life in the Psalms where we find nothing but "the expressions and breathings of devout and holy affections; such as an humble and fervent love to God, admiration of his glorious perfections and wonderful works, earnest desires, thirstings and pantings of soul after God, delight and joy in God, a sweet and melting gratitude to God for his great goodness, an holy exultation and triumph of soul in the favor, sufficiency and faithfulness of God, his love to, and delight in the saints, the excellent of the earth, his great delight in the Word and ordinances of God, his grief for his own and others' sins, and his fervent zeal for God, and against the enemies of God and his church."

But these affections are not merely private passions; the psalms were written for God's people to use in public worship and are suited to express the religion and spirituality of all God's people.

Consider the apostle Paul, who was clearly full of heartfelt affection. He was, in the course of his life, "inflamed, actuated and entirely swallowed up, by a most ardent love to his glorious Lord, esteeming all things as loss, for the excellency of the knowledge of him, and esteeming them but dung that he might win him. He represents himself as overpowered by this holy affection, and as it were compelled by it to go forward in his service, through all difficulties and sufferings."

Throughout Paul's letters we read of his overflowing affection for the people of God, of a love that can be compared to that of a nursing mother toward her children (see 1 Thess. 2:7–8). He speaks of his "bowels of love" (see Phil. 1:8; Philem. 12, 20), his pity, mercy, and tender care for the people to whom he writes (see 2 Cor. 2:4). Paul agonized in his soul over them (see Col. 2:1) and his heart was "enlarged" toward them (see 2 Cor. 6:11). He often spoke of his affectionate and longing desires (see 1 Thess. 2:8; Rom. 1:11; Phil. 1:8), his great joy (see Phil. 4:10; Philem. 7), his glorying in tribulation (see 2 Thess. 1:4; Rom. 5:3), his hope (see Phil. 1:20) and earnest expectation, as well as godly jealousy (see 2 Cor. 11:2–3).

Indeed, "if anyone can consider these accounts given in the Scripture of this great Apostle, and which he gives of himself, and yet not see that his religion consisted much in affection, [he] must have a strange faculty of managing his eyes, to shut out the light which shines most full in his face."

Yet another who displayed like affections was John. "It is evident by all his writings . . . that he was a person remarkably full of affection: his addresses to those whom he wrote to, [were] inexpressibly tender and pathetical, breathing nothing but the most fervent love, as though he were all made up of sweet and holy affection."

And then, of course, there is Jesus himself, "a person who was remarkably of a tender and affectionate heart," a man whose "virtue was expressed very much in the exercise of holy affections. He was the greatest instance of ardency, vigor and strength of love, to both God and man, that ever was." Jesus prayed with loud crying and tears and experienced heart-wrenching grief and sorrow. His zeal was prophesied in the Old Testament (see John 2:17), and he felt anger over the sins of others (see Mark 3:5). He wept aloud and openly (see Luke 19:41–42; 13:34). His earnest desires (see Luke 22:15) and pity and compassion (see Matt. 15:32; Luke 7:13) are evident.

If there be any doubt, after all this, that holy affections are the center of the truly spiritual life, one need only recall that the religion of heaven is characterized by heartfelt affections. We consider heaven because the most effective way to learn the true nature of an experience is to examine it where it is found in its purity and perfection. "There is doubtless true religion in heaven, and true religion in its utmost purity and perfection. But according to the Scripture representation of the heavenly state, the religion of heaven consists chiefly in holy and mighty love and joy, and the expression of these in most fervent and exalted praises."

The fact that those in heaven do not as yet have physical bodies demonstrates yet again that bodily manifestations and postures and sensations are not the essence of affections "but the effect of them." There is a "sensation of the mind which loves and rejoices, that is antecedent to any effects on the fluids of the body; and this sensation of the mind, therefore, don't depend on these motions in the body, and so may be in the soul without the body. And wherever there are the exercises of love and joy, there is that sensation of the mind, whether it be in the body, or out; and that inward sensation, or kind of spiritual sense, or feeling, and motion of the soul, is what is called affection."

If we can learn anything from Scripture about the nature of heaven and the experience of the saints there, it is that they have a love and joy that "is exceeding great and vigorous, impressing the heart with the strongest and most lively sensation, of inexpressible sweetness, mightily moving, animating, and engaging them, making them like to a flame of fire. And if such love and joy be not affections, then the word 'affection' is of no use in language. Will any say that the saints in heaven, in beholding the face of their Father, and the glory of their Redeemer, and contemplating his wonderful works, and particularly his laying down his life for them, have their hearts nothing moved and affected, by all which they behold or consider?"

We can only conclude, then, from pervasive scriptural testimony, the lives of saints, [the life of] Jesus himself, and the experience of those in heaven, that true spirituality and godly religion consist, in large part, in the enjoyment of sanctified affections.

4

THE AFFECTIONS IN PRAYER, PRAISE, AND PREACHING

THAT HOLY AFFECTIONS ARE the essence of true spirituality can also be seen from what God has commanded concerning prayer and public worship.

We are not to pray as if our petitions inform God of what he doesn't know or change his mind or prevail on him to bestow mercy that he was otherwise disinclined to give. Rather we pray "to affect our own hearts with the things we express, and so to prepare us to receive the blessings we ask." In fact, virtually all external expressions of worship "can be of no further use, than as they have some tendency to affect our own hearts, or the hearts of others."

Consider, for example, the singing of praises to God, which seem to be "appointed wholly to excite and express religious affections. No other reason can be assigned, why we should express ourselves to God in verse, rather than in prose, and do it with music, but only that such is our nature and frame, that these things have a tendency to move our affections."

Some actually orchestrate worship in such a way that the affections of the heart are reined in and, in some cases, even suppressed. People often fear the external manifestation of internal zeal and love and desire and joy. Though they sing, they do so in a way that the end in view is the mere articulation of words and declaration of truths. But if that were what God intended, why did he not ordain that we recite, in prose, biblical truths about him? Why sing? It can't be simply for the aesthetic value of music or because of the pleasure it brings, for that would turn worship manward, as if we were now the focus rather than God. We sing because God has created not only our minds but also our hearts and souls, indeed our bodies as well, in such a way that music elicits and intensifies holy affections for God and facilitates their lively and vigorous expression.

The same may be said of how God operates on our souls in the preaching of his Word. Books and commentaries and the like provide us with "good doctrinal or speculative understanding of the things of the Word of God, yet they have not an equal tendency to impress them on men's hearts and affections." So with a view to "affecting" sinners and not merely "informing" them, God has appointed that his Word be applied in a particularly lively way through preaching.

Therefore, when we think of how public worship should be constructed and what methods should be employed in the praise of God and the edification of his people, "such means are to be desired, as have much of a tendency to move the affections. Such books, and such a way of preaching the Word, and administration of ordinances, and such a way of worshiping God in prayer, and singing praises, is much to be desired, as has a tendency deeply to affect the hearts of those who attend these means."

When people object that certain styles of public worship seem especially chosen for their capacity to awaken and intensify and express the affections of the heart, they should be told that such is precisely the God-ordained purpose of worship. What they fear—namely, the heightening and deepening of the heart's desire and love for God, and the expansion and increase of the soul's delight and joy in God, what they typically call "emotionalism" or even "manipulation"—is the very goal of worship itself. For God is most glorified in his people when their hearts are most satisfied (i.e., when they are most "affected" with joy) in him.[1]

Some would say that it isn't the joy or love or desire to which they object, but the external manifestations, whether in weeping or celebration or bodily movement, that such affections so often produce. But as we have noted, God created us as a union of body and spirit such that alterations in the latter, whether growth in understanding or illumination of the Word, invariably affect the former. More on this later.

---

[1]See John Piper, *Desiring God* (Sisters, Ore.: Multnomah, 2003).

So much does true spirituality consist in affections that one may say "that without holy affection there is no true religion: and no light in the understanding is good, which don't produce holy affection in the heart; no habit or principle in the heart is good, which has no such exercise; and no external fruit is good, which don't proceed from such exercises."

There is a lot of "religion" in the world, together with its anticipated rituals, rites, gestures, beliefs, acts of moral virtue, and charity, as well as organizations and institutions and traditions designed to perpetuate and promote it, ostensibly to the glory of God. But without holy affections, all such activities and the effort to advertise them are nothing but wind. Those who insist on the intellect of man or the doctrinal accuracy of his thoughts as the pinnacle of religious expression need to consider that *no idea or attitude or theory or doctrine is of any value that does not inflame the heart and stir the affections in love and joy and fear of God*. Those who argue that moral obedience is the essence of religion fail to see that such behavior is only good to the degree that it springs from and finds its source in the holy affections of the heart as they are described in Scripture.

Yet another proof of this is the scriptural portrayal of *hardness of heart* as the essence of sin and moral rebellion (see Mark 3:5; Rom. 2:5; Ezek. 3:7; Ps. 95:7–10; 2 Chron. 36:13; Isa. 63:17). "Now by a hard heart, is plainly meant an unaffected heart, or a heart not easy to be moved with virtuous affections, like a stone, insensible, stupid, unmoved and hard to be impressed. Hence the hard heart is called a stony heart, and is opposed to an heart of flesh, that has feeling, and is sensibly touched and moved."

Scripture is also clear that a "tender" heart is the one that "is easily impressed by what ought to affect it." For example, God commended Josiah because his heart was tender, by which he surely meant that his heart was "easily moved with religious and pious affection" (see 2 Kings 22:19).

Negative reactions to this argument are to some extent understandable. Many point to those who in a season of revival or renewal allowed their zeal and affections to lead them into error. Others experienced high affections but produced little fruit and even appeared to have "returned like the dog to his vomit." But to dismiss affection altogether as having little if anything to do with true spirituality is simply an example of moving from one extreme to another. It is as much an error to dismiss affections entirely as unimportant to the reality of true religion as it is to focus on high affections without regard to their source or nature. Satan is happy with either error. He would as much have us fall into a lifeless formality as he would that we be stirred and energized by affections unrelated to truth.

We must never forget that whereas there is more to true spirituality or religion than affections, "yet true religion consists so much in the affections, that there can be no true religion without them. *He who has no religious affection, is in a state of spiritual death, and is wholly destitute of the powerful, quickening, saving influences of the Spirit of God upon his heart.* As there is no true religion where there is nothing else but affection, so there is no true religion where there is no religious affection. As on the one hand, there must be light in the understanding, as well as an affected fervent heart; where there is heat without light, there can be nothing divine or heavenly in that heart; so on the other hand, where there is a kind of light without heat, a head stored with notions and speculations, with a cold and unaffected heart, there can be nothing divine in that light; that knowledge is no true spiritual knowledge of divine things. *If the great things of religion are rightly understood, they will affect the heart.* The reason why men are not affected by such infinitely great, important, glorious, and wonderful things, as they often hear and read of, in the Word of God, is undoubtedly because they are blind. If they were not so, it would be impossible, and utterly inconsistent with human nature, that their hearts should be otherwise than strongly impressed, and greatly moved by such things."

The fact that a person has much affection doesn't prove he is truly spiritual. But if that individual has no affection it most assuredly proves he has no true religion. "The right way, is not to reject all affections, nor to approve all; but to distinguish between affections, approving some, and rejecting others; separating between the wheat and the chaff, the gold and the dross, the precious and the vile."

If our thesis is correct, and true spirituality lies in the experience, enjoyment, and expression of holy affections, it is to our shame that we are no more affected with the great truths of Scripture than we are.

This is especially the case when we consider how profoundly moved and affected people are by worldly things that have little if anything to do with God and the revelation of himself in the face of Jesus Christ. And yet how common it is among men "that their affections are much more exercised and engaged in other matters, than in religion! In things which concern men's worldly interest, their outward delights, their honor and reputation, and their natural relations, they have their desires eager, their appetites vehement, their love warm and affectionate, their zeal ardent; in these things their hearts are tender and sensible, easily moved, deeply impressed, much concerned, very sensibly affected, and greatly engaged; much depressed with grief at worldly losses, and highly raised with joy at worldly successes and prosperity. But how insensible and unmoved are most men, about the great things of another world! How dull are their affections! How heavy and hard their hearts in these matters! Here their love is cold, their desires languid, their zeal low, and their gratitude small.

"How they can sit and hear of the infinite height, and depth, and length, and breadth of the love of God in Christ Jesus, of his giving his infinitely dear Son, to be offered up a sacrifice for the sins of men, and of the unparalleled love of the innocent, and holy, and tender Lamb of God, manifested in his dying agonies, his bloody sweat, his loud and bitter cries, and bleeding heart, and all this for enemies, to redeem them from deserved, eternal burnings, and to bring to unspeakable and everlasting joy and glory; and yet be cold, and heavy, insensible, and regardless! Where are the exercises of our affections proper, if not here? What is it that does more require them? And what can be a fit occasion of their lively and vigorous exercise, if not such a one as this? Can anything be set in our view, greater and more important? Anything more wonderful and surprising? Or more nearly concerning our interest? Can we suppose the wise Creator implanted such principles in the human nature as the affections, to be of use to us, and to be exercised on certain proper occasions, but to lie still on such an occasion as this? Can any Christian who believes the truth of these things, entertain such thoughts?"

If ever there were occasion for the exercise of human affection, it would be in regard to those things or objects that are most worthy of our energy and joy and delight. "But is there anything which Christians can find in heaven or earth, so worthy to be the objects of their admiration and love, their earnest and longing desires, their hope, and their rejoicing, and their fervent zeal, as those things that are held forth to us in the gospel of Jesus Christ? In which not only are things declared most worthy to affect us, but they are exhibited in the most affecting manner. The glory and beauty of the blessed Jehovah, which is most worthy in itself, to be the object of our admiration and love, is there exhibited in the most affecting manner that can be conceived of, as it appears, shining in all its luster, in the face of an incarnate, infinitely loving, meek, compassionate, dying Redeemer. All the virtues of the Lamb of God, his humility, patience, meekness, submission, obedience, love and compassion, are exhibited to our view, in a manner the most tending to move our affections, of any that can be imagined; as they all had their greatest trial, and their highest exercise, and so their brightest manifestation, when he was in the most affecting circumstances; even when he was under his last sufferings, those unutterable and unparalleled sufferings he endured, from his tender love and pity to us.

"There also the hateful nature of our sins is manifested in the most affecting manner possible: as we see the dreadful effects of them, in that our Redeemer, who undertook to answer for us, suffered for them. And there we have the most affecting manifestation of God's hatred of sin, and his wrath and justice in punishing it; as we see his justice in the strictness and inflexibleness of it; and his wrath in its terribleness, in so dreadfully punishing our sins, in one who was infinitely dear to him, and loving to us. So has God disposed things, in the affair of our redemption, and in his glorious dispensations, revealed to us in the gospel, *as though everything were purposely contrived in such a manner, as to have the greatest possible tendency to reach our hearts in the most tender part, and move our affections most sensibly and strongly.* How great cause have we therefore to be humbled to the dust, that we are no more affected!"

5

"SIGNS"
OF NOTHING (1)

SOME WHO HAVE READ the previous chapters may be inclined to say, "I'm certainly not among those who lack spiritual affections. I am often greatly moved and stirred by spiritual truths." But the mere presence of intense and heartfelt affections is itself no proof that one is the object of the saving activity of God's Spirit. We must be diligent to distinguish between affections that are genuine and God-given and those that are not.

In this chapter we will begin to look at those things to which people often appeal as evidence of the authenticity of spiritual life but which, in fact, prove nothing. In other words, there are some experiences that prove neither that one is the recipient of divine grace nor that one is not. People who testify of the following may well be children of God. But they may as easily not be. So let's begin.

(1) Nothing is known for sure from the fact that affections are intense or are raised high in the heart of the person.

Of course, there are some who say that affections have nothing at all to do with genuine spirituality. They simply write them off as delusional or fanatical. But if what we've seen thus far is true, authentic spirituality will produce intense affections of heart and mind. "If true religion in the hearts of men be raised a great height, divine and holy affections will be raised to a great height." In other words, whereas the existence of heightened affections does not itself prove the reality of one's religious confession, the absence of affections certainly proves its falsity.

Consider, by way of example, those countless occasions in Scripture where Christians are commended for their love for God or hatred of sin or gratitude for saving mercy or are described as having strong desires for God. Are these not spiritual affections? If they are, who would argue that they could ever be exercised with too great intensity? Who would argue that his affections are sufficiently great, that he has no need to grow and deepen in his passion for God? Who would dare say that he is affected enough with the wonderful love of God to sinners or would dare pray that he might not be affected any more than he already is, because "high affections are improper, and very unlovely in Christians, being enthusiastical, and ruinous to true religion?"

Scripture often commands us to experience the highest of spiritual affections, such as loving God with all our heart, soul, mind, and strength (see Matt. 22:34–40). We are to rejoice and be exceedingly glad (see Matt. 5:12; cf. Ps. 68:3). Indeed, we are to "leap for joy" (Luke 6:23; cf. Ps. 21:1; 63:3–7; 71:23). The psalmist speaks of his love as if it were unspeakably great (see Ps. 119:97) and his hatred of sin as powerful and perfect (see Ps. 139:21–22). He speaks of his sorrow for sin and his hunger for God (see Ps. 119:53, 136) in the same way.

Earlier we noted how the apostle Paul often expressed powerful affections of pity and concern for others, anguish of heart, fervent and abundant love, earnest longing, exceeding joy, intense expectation and hope, overflowing tears, travail of soul, grief, godly jealousy, and zeal.

This is especially true of the saints in heaven, who experience the depths of genuine spiritual life far exceeding anything we know on earth. "They are all as a pure heavenly flame of fire in their love and in the greatness and strength of their joy and gratitude; their praises are represented, 'as the voice of many waters, and as the voice of a great thunder.' Now the only reason why their affections are so much higher than the holy affections of saints on earth is [that] they see the things they are affected by, more according to their truth, and have their affections more conformed to the nature of things. And therefore, if religious affections in men here below are . . . of the same nature and kind with theirs, the higher they are, and the nearer they are to theirs in degree the better; because therein they will be so much the more conformed to truth, as theirs are."

We can only conclude that they are in great error who condemn people as fanatical and deluded merely because their affections are intense and powerful.

On the other hand, it is equally important to note that the intensity of spiritual affections is *not* infallible proof that they are of a saving and gracious nature. Both the Old and New Testaments often speak of people who were deeply affected with error. The Israelites at the Red Sea enthusiastically sang God's praises, only later to forget his mighty works and abandon him. No sooner had they rejoiced at Sinai than they turned to build a golden calf. People who were greatly moved at the resurrection of Lazarus and provided Jesus with shouts of joy and praise at his triumphal entry, later replaced their "Hosanna! Hosanna!" with "Crucify! Crucify!"

The point is this: whereas true spirituality will always manifest itself in powerful and intense affections, the latter alone are not proof that one is regenerate.

(2) Nothing is known for sure when the affections of the heart have a great influence on the body.

All affections, to some degree or other, have an impact on the body. As noted earlier, "Such is our nature, and such are the laws of union of soul and body, that the mind can have no lively or vigorous exercise, without some effect upon the body. So subject is the body to the mind, and so much do its fluids, especially the animal spirits, attend the motions and exercises of the mind, that there can't be so much as an intense thought, without an effect upon them. Yea, 'tis questionable, whether an embodied soul ever so much as thinks one thought, or has any exercise at all, but that there is some corresponding motion or alteration of motion, in some degree, of the fluids, in some part of the body." This would imply that the greater the affection, the greater will be its influence on the body.

But we should *not* conclude from this that bodily manifestations are *always* infallible evidence that affections are spiritual or saving. After all, such physiological effects are often the result of affections arising from temporal or worldly or even fleshly interests. Our hearts are often greatly engaged by sinful pursuits that have the power of bearing on the body.

There simply isn't anything in Scripture or in reason that would lead us to think that being greatly affected with a view of God's glory should *not* cause the body to faint or shake or otherwise be moved. We earlier looked at Peter's description of "joy unspeakable and full of glory" (1 Pet. 1:8, KJV). "And who that considers what man's nature is, and what the nature of the affections are, can reasonably doubt but that such unutterable and glorious joys, may be too great and mighty for weak dust and ashes, so as to be considerably overbearing to it? It is evident by the Scripture, that true divine discoveries, or ideas of God's glory, when given in a great degree, have a tendency, by affecting the mind, to overbear the body; because the Scripture teaches us often, that if these ideas or views should be given to such a degree, as they are given in heaven, the weak frame of the body could not subsist under it, and that no man can, in that manner, see God and live."

Let's look at a few biblical examples. In Psalm 84:2 we read, "My soul longeth, yea, even fainteth for the courts of the LORD, my heart and my flesh crieth out for the living God" (KJV). In Psalm 63:1 the psalmist declares that his soul "thirsteth for thee, my flesh longeth for thee in a dry and thirsty land, where no water is" (KJV). Habakkuk speaks of his body being overcome with a sense of the majesty of God. His belly trembled, his lips quivered, and a feeling of rottenness filled his bones (see Hab. 3:16; cf. Psalm 119:120). In Daniel 10:8–9 we see that the prophet lost his physical strength and fell to the ground as dead. So, too, was the experience of John the apostle (see Rev. 1:17).

We should also note how often Scripture makes use of bodily manifestations to describe the strength of spiritual affections, such as trembling (see Ps. 119:120; Ezra 9:4; Isa. 66:2, 5; Hab. 3:16), groaning (see Rom. 8:26), being sick (see Song 2:5; 5:8), singing for joy (see Ps. 84:2), panting (see Ps. 38:10; 42:1; 119:131), and fainting (see Ps. 84:2; 119:81). Obviously God regarded these expressions as appropriate to represent the degree and intensity of affection. Indeed, if spiritual affections are alien to such bodily effects and have no tendency to produce such physiological manifestations, and these manifestations are only the delusion of Satan, it is strange that God would use them "to represent the high degree of holy and heavenly affections."

(3) The fact that people are inclined to talk at length about their spiritual experience proves nothing.

When people talk incessantly about the things of God, especially those who used to be shy and virtually silent, some conclude this is sure and certain proof that their conversion was real. Others are just as quick to conclude the opposite. After all, didn't the Pharisees and hypocrites make a show of their claim to spirituality by loudly talking about religious issues and making a public display of their knowledge?

But in neither case can we conclude anything decisively, for Scripture nowhere makes verbal eloquence or its opposite a criterion of true spirituality. It's only natural when someone is deeply affected by something that they speak often of it. But that alone says nothing about whether the affection is of God or of the flesh. Many in the first century were obsessed with religious speech when John the Baptist preached his baptism of repentance, as were others when Jesus performed his miracles. But in neither case were they speaking out of a heart of holy affections.

Clearly, we need something more than mere speech and eloquence and a propensity to talk at length of religious matters before we conclude with any degree of confidence that people are energized by the Holy Spirit.

(4) The way in which people come to have their affections awakened proves nothing about whether those affections are of God or of the flesh.

Many think that the only authentic affections of the heart are those that are awakened in us by the diligent use of those means appointed in Scripture. In other words, they are suspicious of people who testify to deep and profound affections of the heart without being able to account by scriptural means for how they came by them. If people cannot explain rationally how they employed their reason and the means of grace as set forth in Scripture, some judge their alleged affections as false.

Now, on the one hand, an important point of truth is contained in this. It is unbiblical to presume that you will experience the influences of the Spirit if you deliberately ignore and neglect those means outlined in the Word of God. On the other hand, we cannot immediately dismiss the possibility that the Spirit can operate directly on the human heart and it appear to be sovereign and supernatural to the one who is the object of such activity. In other words, the fact that people are unaware of any natural means employed by which the Spirit has exerted gracious influence on their souls does not prove that their resultant affections are false. In fact, God often works in such a way to make it evident that he and he alone is the cause and that people contribute nothing of their own.

A good illustration of this is in Ephesians 1:18–19. There Paul describes how God enlightens the minds of Christians that they might know the mighty power that operates within them. Clearly he envisions them knowing this by experience, which is to say they "feel it, and discern it, and are conscious of it, as sensibly distinguishable from the natural operations of their own minds."

But we must also acknowledge that merely experiencing what one believes is a direct and sovereign influence of the Spirit does not prove that such is the case. People often say, "I didn't produce this affection. I did nothing to create it, so it must be from God." We have to consider the possibility that "what they have been the subjects of may, indeed, not be from themselves directly, but may be from the operation of an invisible agent, some spirit besides their own: but it does not thence follow, that it was from the Spirit of God. There are other spirits who have influence on the minds of men, besides the Holy Ghost."

Even if we concede that it is God's Spirit who exerts such influences on the heart, they may not be redemptive or saving in nature but rather may be a manifestation of the "common grace" of God. The Spirit can convict of sin and influence the mind of a person without him having any saving intent.

And finally, we have to reckon with the fact that some people are physiologically and emotionally of such a constitution that they are easily given to subjective experiences and imaginations and strong affections that come neither from the Holy Spirit nor from the Enemy. The point is simply this: how one comes by a religious affection, whether or not one has employed particular means or senses a spontaneous influence from without, proves *nothing* either way about the spiritual authenticity or origin of it. We need something more to make such a judgment.

(5) When people experience religious affections because a Scripture text suddenly came to mind, it proves nothing.

God can use a biblical passage to awaken a powerful experience in the soul. But the fact that such experiences are attended by or are the fruit of such inspired texts does not itself prove that God is the author of them. No matter how suddenly or unexpectedly the memory of such biblical texts may arise, no matter how emotional or moving their effect may be, this alone does not guarantee that it came from God. The Bible simply never gives us explicit instruction on this point.

The objection of those who have had such experiences is that, since the Bible is pure and true and perfect, any affections arising in conjunction with it must be of God. But we must remember that "affections may arise on *occasion* of the Scripture, and not *properly come from* the Scripture, as the genuine fruit of the Scripture, and by a right use of it, but from an abuse of it." After all, "what evidence is there that the devil can't bring texts of Scripture to the mind, and misapply them, to deceive persons?" Satan used biblical texts in his attempt to lead Jesus into sin in the wilderness. If he did it with Jesus, what reason do we have for doubting that he might do similarly with us?

Again, let's not jump to unwarranted conclusions. This does not suggest that the Spirit cannot or does not make us conscious of particular biblical texts or truths. But neither does the presence of a biblical text in our minds prove that it was awakened by the Spirit. A person's affections can be greatly aroused and stirred by biblical texts coming to mind with vivid and overwhelming power. But we need more than this alone to prove that it was the work of the Holy Spirit and not an evil spirit, or perhaps even the natural operations of the human spirit.

(6) The mere fact that certain religious affections are characterized by love is no proof that the Holy Spirit is their author.

Of course, love is the preeminent Christian virtue, and no one would deny that where it is absent so too is the Spirit. But neither should we conclude that the existence of love proves that the Spirit is present.

Every Christian virtue, even love, has its demonic or fleshly counterfeit. Scripture often speaks of people feeling love in their hearts when it is evident there is no saving grace in it (see Matt. 24:12–13).

The apostle Paul seems to intimate that there were many in his day who had a counterfeit love for Christ, for he speaks a blessing of grace in Ephesians 6:24 (KJV) on "all them that love our Lord Jesus Christ in sincerity. . . ." Would he have spoken in these terms were it not possible for some to experience a form of "love" that lacked sincerity? Paul was aware that "there were many who had a kind of love to Christ, whose love was not pure and spiritual."

(7) Often people experience a wide variety of religious affections
that seem naturally to accompany one another.
But this proves nothing as to the spiritual origin of them.

We've already noted that virtually every spiritual affection has its counterfeit, whether that be sorrow for sin or the fear of God or reverence or gratitude or joy or earnest desires of the heart. It stands to reason that a person may experience any number of such false affections simultaneously or one following after the other. Those who witnessed Jesus raise Lazarus from the dead, although they later proved to be unbelievers, displayed admiration and love for Jesus in view of what he had accomplished. There was a measure of reverence and gratitude in their hearts and they joyfully praised him with loud voices. Yet there was nothing saving or gracious in the affections of their hearts.

6

"SIGNS"
OF NOTHING (2)

WE ARE CONSIDERING those "signs" or experiences in the life of individuals which prove nothing concerning the authenticity of their spiritual state. So let's continue.

(8) The order or sequence in which one experiences religious affections proves nothing certain about their origin or nature.

Does Scripture teach a particular sequence from conviction of sin to assurance of salvation? In other words, is it always the case when God is savingly at work in the human soul that a person will first experience deep pains of conscience, followed by a sense of humiliation for having failed God, only after which comes that comfort and joy which are the fruit of forgiveness?

There are undoubtedly countless examples in Scripture where this "order" or "scheme" is characteristic of God's people. Both in his dealings with corporate Israel as well as in his work in the individual heart, it makes sense that "before God delivers persons from a state of sin and exposedness to eternal destruction, he should give them some considerable sense of the evil he delivers from; that they may be delivered sensibly, and understand their own salvation, and know something of what God does for them."

On the other hand, it would be unjustified to conclude that joy is always genuine simply because it follows upon the fear of hell. There is a great difference between being terrified of eternal condemnation and experiencing conviction of conscience for having sinned against

an infinitely holy God. Numerous individuals "have frightful apprehensions of hell, a dreadful pit ready to swallow them up, and flames
just ready to lay hold of them, and devils around them ready to seize
them; who at the same time seem to have very little proper enlightenings of conscience, really convincing them of their sinfulness of heart
and life. The devil, if permitted, can terrify men as well as the Spirit
of God."

The point is that if Satan can counterfeit those affections that are
the *result* of the saving and gracious operations of the Spirit, he can
also counterfeit those experiences that are *preparatory to* the reception
of saving grace.

Due to differences in personality and temperament, some people
are more prone than others to react to perceptions of hell and judgment. In other words, the imaginations of some are more vivid and
easily stirred at the thought of impending judgment and the horrors
of hell. Thus the mere experience of such fears is no proof that such
people are recipients of the Spirit's saving operations.

Even on those occasions when the Spirit is the one responsible
for people reacting in fear of hell and judgment, the joy of forgiveness
will not necessarily follow. Men and women can quench the Spirit's
work and in turn produce for and in themselves a hope and a joy that
is grounded in something other than the efficacy of the saving work
of Jesus.

The Spirit's work is mysterious and varied and subject only to
the sovereign pleasure of his own will. What we must be concerned
with is the *nature* of what God has produced in the soul and not the
Spirit's *method* of producing it. So, in summary, the sequence or steps
or perceived causal relation of various spiritual experiences proves
little, perhaps nothing at all, concerning the origin and nature of what
has happened. For that proof we need to attend to what Scripture has
explicitly set forth as true signs of true affections.

*(9) One might think that fervency in the normal affairs of worship
and religious duty would be a sure sign of gracious affections.
But this is not the case.*

Once again, we cannot deny that those who are graciously and savingly
influenced by the Spirit will invariably enjoy reading Scripture and

praying and singing God's praise. They most assuredly will! We can even say that a person who neglects the standard expressions of piety and zeal for the Lord has no basis on which to claim that he or she is the recipient of God's saving presence.

Consider several well-known examples in Scripture. Anna's life was characterized by fasting and unceasing prayer (see Luke 2:37). Those in the early church were together on a daily basis, sharing table fellowship and praising God (see Acts 2:46–47). Daniel and David were faithful to give themselves to thrice-daily prayer (see Ps. 55:17). And nothing is more characteristic of authentic spiritual affections than joy in the worship and celebration of God (see Ps. 26:8; 27:4; 84:1–2; 89:15; 135:3; 147:1).

But "persons being disposed to abound and to be zealously engaged in the external exercises of religion, and to spend much time in them, is no sure evidence of grace; because such a disposition is found in many that have no grace." This was certainly the case with many in Israel (see Isa. 1:2–15) as well as with the Pharisees in the days of Jesus.

So, whereas the chronic absence of fervent prayer and praise and fellowship (just to mention a few expressions of zeal) is an indication that a profession of faith is likely spurious, the mere presence of such activities is not sufficient to prove that one's professed faith is gracious and saving in nature.

(10) Not even the vocal praise of God is a sure and certain sign of gracious affections.

This is an extension of the previous point but with a focus on that one activity that many consider infallible proof of the Spirit's influence. Again, no one will deny that those who are truly saved will love to sing the praises of their Lord and Master. But singing praises is not sufficient to prove that Christ is indeed their Savior. There are simply too many instances in Scripture where people "praise" and "glorify" God but are bereft of his saving operations.

Many praised Jesus on the performance of his miracles, yet time revealed they knew nothing of him in a saving way (see Mark 2:12; Matt. 9:8; 15:31; Luke 4:15; 5:26; 7:16; Acts 4:21).

(11) Merely having a deep and profound assurance that one is saved proves nothing about the authenticity of one's faith.

Some argue that there is no such thing as full and confident assurance of salvation. Therefore, those who profess to have experienced it demonstrate that they have not as yet tasted saving grace.

Most, however, concede that there are numerous instances in the Scriptures where true believers are said to have an assurance of salvation (see Job 19:25). One also thinks of the countless times in the Psalms where David spoke without hesitation and in the most positive manner possible of his relationship with God. Numerous times in the Upper Room Discourse Jesus went out of his way to assure his disciples of the certainty of their inheritance and the assurance of peace with God (see John 15:11; 16:33). Such declarations are also found in Paul's writings (see Gal. 2:20; Phil. 1:21; 2 Tim. 1:12; 4:8; Heb. 6:17–18).

But once more we must point out that merely having assurance of salvation and a confident peace of mind and heart is not an infallible proof that one is accepted of God. Those who loudly and without the slightest doubt declare the certainty of their relationship with God may be like the Pharisees "who never doubted but that they were saints, and the most eminent of saints, and were bold to go to God, and come up near to him, and lift up their eyes, and thank him for the great distinction he had made between them and other men."

The unregenerate heart is quite capable of self-deception, self-flattery, and a self-confidence that leads it to heartily assert its safety with God. True believers embrace the assurance of salvation with humility and caution, whereas the false assert it with a brazen confidence that borders on arrogant presumption. True believers, unlike hypocrites, are also keenly aware of their own sin and the potential it has for leading them into a false sense of security. It is also the case that Satan will leave a hypocrite undisturbed in his false assurance (and perhaps even embolden him in it), whereas he may constantly attack the born-again believer lest the power of hope in his heart strengthen his commitment to holiness and purity of life. The hypocrite "looks clean and bright in his own eyes" while the true saint is made ever more aware of his failings and corruption.

The grounds for this false assurance can vary from self-congratulation that comes from the diligent performance of religious external duties to that sense of self-righteousness that follows from having allegedly received revelations from God or feeling the subjective impression of a Scripture text spontaneously brought to mind. Regardless of what one thinks about the validity of such extra-biblical "revelations" and "impressions," they are not the biblical grounds for assurance of salvation. Many who have never "heard" from God in this manner arrogantly think they have and base their confidence of eternal life on that alone.

Those who have truly been born of God maintain their assurance "by the soul's being kept in a holy frame, and grace maintained in lively exercise. If the actings of grace do much decay in the Christian, and he falls into a lifeless frame, he loses his assurance. But this kind of confidence of hypocrites will not be shaken by sin. They (at least some of them), will maintain their boldness in their hope, in the most corrupt frames and wicked ways, which is a sure evidence of their delusion."

Some actually revel in their assurance of salvation in spite of the absence of gracious works and godly obedience and a knowledge of God as revealed in Christ. They claim that this is what the Scripture means when it speaks of "living" or "walking by faith" and "not by sight." But the Bible knows nothing of "any such faith in Christ or the operation of God, that is not founded in a spiritual sight of Christ."

Some imagine that "living by faith" means believing you are saved even though there is no evidence in life or experience of ever having encountered the light of the glory of God in the face of Jesus Christ. You are simply to "believe" and "trust" that your relationship with God is good in spite of there being no evidence—or even having all evidence to the contrary. Thus he who believes he is saved despite all evidence to the contrary is honored as one who has extraordinary faith.

Of course, it is true that we are to trust in God and maintain our faith even when times are confusing and dark and there appears no evidence of his presence or activity. He may seem distant and dull to our prayers, and his providence may frown upon our best efforts. "But how different a thing is this from trusting in God without spiritual sight, and being at the same time in a dead and carnal frame!"

That some Christians fall into doubt regarding the state of their souls is not always a bad thing. Their failure to believe and trust in the certainty of their salvation is not a failure of faith on their part but a merciful gift from God. "For so hath God contrived and constituted things, in his dispensations towards his own people, that when their love decays, and the exercises of it fail, or become weak, fear should arise; for then they need it to restrain them from sin, and to excite 'em to care for the good of their souls, and so to stir them up to watchfulness and diligence in religion. But God hath so ordered that when love rises, and is in vigorous exercise, then fear should vanish, and be driven away."

In summary, people "directly thwart God's wise and gracious constitution of things, who exhort others to be confident in their hope when in dead frames; under a notion of living by faith, and not by sight, and trusting God in the dark, and living upon Christ, and not upon experiences; and warn them not to doubt of their good estate, lest they should be guilty of the dreadful sin of unbelief. And it has a direct tendency to establish the most presumptuous hypocrites, and to prevent their ever calling their state in question, how much soever wickedness rages, and reigns in their hearts, and prevails in their lives, under a notion of honoring God, by hoping against hope, and confidently trusting in God, when things look very dark."

(12) That true Christians are impressed by the external behavior and attracted to the lifestyle of another person proves nothing concerning the nature of the latter's religious affections.

The fact is, true believers do not have the necessary discernment to determine who is and who is not saved. They may know in their own souls the reality of saving grace, but this is something they can neither feel nor see in the heart of another. We can at best observe others' behavior, "but the Scripture plainly intimates that this way of judging what is in men by outward appearances, is at best uncertain and liable to deceit." This is confirmed by God's word to Samuel: "Do not look on his appearance or on the height of his stature, because I have rejected him. For the LORD sees not as man sees: man looks on the outward appearance, but the LORD looks on the heart" (1 Sam. 16:7; see also Isa. 11:3).

When people give what appears to be external evidence of internal life, it is our responsibility to receive them cordially into fellowship and to love them and rejoice with them as brothers and sisters of Christ. But even then it is possible for us to be deceived as to their true spiritual condition. As we have seen repeatedly in this discussion, people may display a wide range of virtues and religious affections and yet be without a spark of saving grace in their hearts. They may express love for God, admire his attributes, and feel sorrow for sin, yet be devoid of true spiritual life. They may abase themselves in what appears to be godly humility and manifest reverence, submission, gratitude, joy, religious longings, and zeal for the good of other folk, yet know nothing of the forgiving mercy of God.

Such people may experience these affections in the same order and sequence as do those who are truly the recipients of saving grace, yet remain in spiritual death. They may weep and tremble and fall to the ground under what appears to be the weight of some vision or sense of God's goodness to them, yet be lost. They may speak fluently and fervently of spiritual matters and how Scripture texts and redemptive promises have come spontaneously to mind, leading them to loudly praise and glorify God and to call upon others to praise him for showing grace to such unworthy sinners. Such affections may lead them into every conceivable religious endeavor, such as prayer and study of the Word and singing and attending theological conferences.

Yet, notwithstanding such experiences and professions of faith, "it has been made plain, that there may be all these things, and yet there be nothing more than the common [or non-redemptive, non-saving] influences of the Spirit of God, joined with the delusions of Satan, and the wicked and deceitful heart." One can add to all of this that a person may have a sweet personality and a solid grasp of biblical doctrine and a capacity to dialogue with other saints on the glories and subtleties of Christian faith, and yet be void of saving grace. "How great therefore may the resemblance be, as to all outward expressions and appearances, between a hypocrite and a true saint! Doubtless 'tis the glorious prerogative of the omniscient God, as the great searcher of hearts, to be able well to separate between sheep and goats."

It is perfectly understandable why a true believer would be quick to affirm the salvation of another who testifies to having experienced God's saving influence. When a person uses biblical vocabulary to describe in passionate and articulate terms what appears to be the same experience of a regenerate man or woman, and does so with great delight, joy, and confidence, it makes sense that a Christian would rejoice in what he or she hears. After all, "a true saint greatly delights in holiness: it is a most beautiful thing in his eyes; and God's work, in savingly renewing and making holy and happy, a poor, and before perishing soul, appears to him a most glorious work. No wonder, therefore, that his heart is touched and greatly affected when he hears another give a probable account of this work, wrought on his own heart, and when he sees in him probable appearances of holiness; whether those pleasing appearances have anything real to answer them or no."

But we must resist the temptation to make premature judgments about the state of another's soul. Those who profess faith in Christ, especially in times of revival and the extraordinary outpouring of the Spirit, are often like the blossoms of spring: "there are vast numbers of them upon the trees which all look fair and promising; but yet very many of them never come to anything. And many of those, that in a little time wither up, and drop off, and rot under the trees; yet for a while, look as beautiful and gay as others; and not only so, but smell sweet and send forth a pleasant odor, so that we can't, by any of our senses, certainly distinguish those blossoms which have in them that secret virtue, which will afterwards appear in the fruit, and that inward solidity and strength which shall enable them to bear and cause them to be perfected by the hot summer sun, that will dry up the others." Thus, and this cannot be stated too strongly, it is "the mature fruit which comes afterwards, and not the beautiful colors and smell of the blossom, that we must judge by."

There is hardly anything more explicit in the teachings of Jesus himself than the rules by which we are to judge the sincerity of someone's profession of faith. We must judge the nature of the tree by the quality of its fruit. But if the fruit of saving virtue is subject to being counterfeited, what good is this as a rule for discerning true from false? The answer is found *not in the mere presence* of what appears to be fruit, but in its *perseverance*. If the fruit shows itself not merely once, no matter how fervently and sweetly, but endures and matures over time and through trial, we can more solidly judge whether they be truly of God (although even then our judgment is still fallible).

7

SIGNS OF AUTHENTIC
AFFECTIONS:
AN INTRODUCTION

LET'S BE CLEAR THAT what we are seeking are "the distinguishing qualifications of those that are in favor with God, and entitled to his eternal rewards." In other words, what is the nature of true spirituality and those distinguishing features in the human soul that are acceptable in the sight of God?

We've spent considerable time demonstrating that the mere presence of intense and heartfelt affections is itself no proof that one is the object of the saving activity of God's Spirit. Clearly we must be careful to differentiate between affections that accompany salvation and those that do not.

In the preceding chapters we focused on twelve things to which people often appeal as evidence of the authenticity of spiritual life. Our aim was to demonstrate that such phenomena and experiences, in fact, prove nothing. There are some experiences that prove neither that one is the recipient of divine grace nor that one is not. People who bear witness to having experienced such things may well be children of God. But they may as easily not be. The manifestations that occur may be the work of the Spirit, but they may as easily not be.

We can now begin describing those signs or criteria by which genuine, saving affections may be known. However, we must keep in mind three things.

First, we must recognize that there never will be a time or system or standard of analysis of such issues that will yield infallible results. To claim that we are able, without error, to determine who is a true believer and who is a hypocrite is to fall prey to the very arrogance we labored in the previous chapters to expose. Yes, God has indeed given signs in Scripture that will help us in this endeavor, but "it was never God's design to give us any rules, by which we may certainly know, who of our fellow professors [i.e., those who profess to have saving faith] are his, and to make a full and clear separation between sheep and goats: but that on the contrary, it was God's design to reserve this to himself, as his prerogative."

Second, we should not expect to find biblical signs that will enable a backslidden person to reassure himself that he is in a good way with God. It is not God's design that such people "should know their good estate: nor is it desirable that they should; but on the contrary, every way best that they should not; and we have reason to bless God, that he has made no provision that such should certainly know the state that they are in, any other way, than by first coming out of the ill frame and way they are in."

The problem isn't with the signs or criteria in God's Word, as if they were intrinsically defective. The problem is with us, to whom the signs are given. We simply lack the clarity and knowledge and objectivity necessary to make an infallible judgment.

It is important to remember that it isn't "God's design that men should obtain assurance [of their salvation] in any other way, than by mortifying corruption, and increasing in grace, and obtaining the lively exercises of it. And although self-examination be a duty of great use and importance, and [is] by no means to be neglected, yet it is not the principal means, by which the saints do get satisfaction of their good estate. Assurance is not to be obtained so much by self-examination, as by action."

This certainly seems to be confirmed by Paul's words in 1 Corinthians 9:26 where he suggests that he "obtained assurance of winning the prize, more by running, than by considering. The swiftness of his pace did more towards his assurance of a conquest, than the strictness of his examination" (see also the exhortation in 2 Pet. 1:5–11).

Third, we should not expect that the signs by which we hope to differentiate between true and false affections will ever prove sufficient to convince those "who have been deceived with great false discoveries and affections, and are once settled in a false confidence, and high conceit of their own supposed great experiences and privileges. Such hypocrites are so conceited of their own wisdom, and so blinded and hardened with a very great self-righteousness (but very subtle and secret, under the disguise of great humility), and so invincible a fondness of their pleasing conceit, of their great exaltation, that it usually signifies nothing at all, to lay before them the most convincing evidences of their hypocrisy."

There are twelve signs by which we hope to distinguish true religious affections from the false. So let's begin. These will be our focus in the coming chapters.

8

THE FIRST SIGN OF
AUTHENTIC AFFECTIONS

Affections that are truly spiritual and gracious, do arise from those influences and operations on the heart, which are spiritual, supernatural and divine.

BEFORE WE CONSIDER THIS first sign, we must begin with an important distinction found repeatedly in Scripture. Some men and women are said to be *spiritual* because the Spirit of God has caused them to be born again and has taken up residence within them as the temple of his abiding presence. Such people are the recipients of those influences of the Spirit that are saving and redemptive. They are partakers of a new, divine nature by virtue of the Spirit's supernatural influence in them. "The Spirit of God so dwells in the hearts of the saints that he there, as a seed or spring of life, exerts and communicates himself in this his sweet and divine nature, making the soul a partaker of God's beauty and Christ's joy, so that the saint has truly fellowship with the Father, and with his Son Jesus Christ, in thus having the communion or participation of the Holy Ghost."

Those whom the Bible calls *natural* men, on the other hand, may well be the objects of the Spirit's influence and activity, but such is not saving or redemptive. Notwithstanding all the gifts and blessings the Spirit may impart, he stops short of the miracle of regeneration. In other words, "though the Spirit of God may many ways influence natural men; yet because it is not thus communicated to them, as an indwelling principle, they don't derive any denomination or character from it; for there being no union, it is not their own."

From this we may conclude that those gracious and saving influences experienced by true believers "are entirely above nature, altogether of a different kind from anything that men find within themselves by nature, or only in the exercise of natural principles." In other words, those gracious affections are from influences that are *supernatural*. It follows, then, that true believers experience "a new inward perception or sensation of their minds, entirely different in its nature and kind, from anything that ever their minds were the subjects of before they were sanctified [i.e., saved]."

The objects of God's saving work experience an entirely new kind of perception that is impossible for mere human nature or human reason or human willpower to produce. It is "a new spiritual sense that the mind has, or a principle of a new kind of perception or spiritual sensation, which is in its whole nature different from any former kinds of sensation of the mind, as tasting is diverse from any of the other senses." This new sense is as different from a merely natural one as the taste of honey is different from the mere idea or description of its flavor.

This "new sense" and the new dispositions that attend it are not new faculties of mind but simply new principles of nature. More specifically, "this new spiritual sense is not a new faculty of understanding, but it is a new foundation laid in the nature of the soul, for a new kind of exercises of the same faculty of understanding. So that new holy disposition of heart that attends this new sense is not a new faculty of will, but a foundation laid in the nature of the soul for a new kind of exercises of the same faculty of will."

The fact that God may reveal to an unsaved and natural man facts that he otherwise didn't know but that he would soon discover through the normal use of his physical senses is no indication that he has received a new spiritual principle. God is doing no more than assisting "natural principles to do the same work to a greater degree, which they do of themselves by nature." But when it comes to the saints, God "operates by infusing or exercising new, divine and supernatural principles; principles which are indeed a new and spiritual nature, and principles vastly more noble and excellent than all that is in natural men."

The point is that people's claims to have "seen" in their minds or "sensed" in their imaginations some idea or spiritual reality, apart from the use of their five senses, proves nothing concerning the origin of such experiences. For example, some claim to have experienced in their imagination or "mind's eye" a great light and take it to be a revelation of the glory of God. Others testify of having "sensed" within themselves the idea of Christ hanging on the cross, or having "seen" him with open arms to receive them, or having had a "lively idea" of Christ on his throne. Some even argue they have "heard" in their minds, apart from the physical sense of hearing with the external ear, Scripture verses or spiritual ideas spoken to them. They believe such experiences are from God "because they say they don't see these things with their bodily eyes, but in their hearts; for they can see them when their eyes are shut." In other words, they think that because these experiences are entirely inward and subjective and vivid, without the aid or use of the five senses, they must be from God.

But none of these experiences is necessarily of God. Anyone can have experiences or ideas or impressions in the imagination like this, even unregenerate folk; one needs no more than what is natural to man to experience them. They don't require regeneration or the Spirit or a new sense of divine things. "A natural man is capable of having an idea, and a lively idea, of shapes and colors and sounds when they are absent, and as capable as a regenerate man is; so there is nothing supernatural in them." Such imaginations or impressions don't require the Holy Spirit and therefore can't be infallible signs of truly gracious and saving affections. Truly gracious affections can be accounted for only by the sovereign and supernatural work of the Spirit and not by human nature alone. In fact, it is often the weakness of mere human nature that accounts for the increase of such impressions.

But when it comes to "a truly spiritual sensation, not only is the manner of its coming into the mind extraordinary, but the sensation itself is totally diverse from all that men have, or can have, in a state of nature, as has been shown." One might still acknowledge that a person can experience such sensations in the mind and imagination, but that the ones that come from the Spirit are different both in their nature and in how they are brought to bear on the human mind.

One cannot deny that God can impart such ideas and impressions on the mind of man. In fact, he did so with Balaam (see Num. 24:16–17). But this is merely the common grace activity of the Spirit, and any affections that arise from such an experience are not necessarily gracious and saving.

Furthermore, Satan himself is capable of suggesting thoughts and words and ideas into the minds of men as a way of tempting them to sin. The false prophets of the Old Testament who claimed to have experienced vivid ideas and images by means of dreams and visions actually received them from Satan (see Deut. 13:1; 1 Kings 22:22; Isa. 28:7; Ezek. 13:7; Zech. 13:4). "And if Satan, or any created being, has power to impress the mind with outward representations, then no particular sort of outward representations can be any evidence of a divine power." Any affections that are built merely on the foundation of such experiences are not spiritual and saving. True and saving affections always come from an undisputed and exclusive divine and supernatural cause.

Certainly the Spirit can make use of Scripture texts that come to mind, if the excellency of what is contained in the texts excites one's affections and not merely the immediate manner in which the texts came to mind. If there is not a new spiritual understanding or sweet sense of the truths in those texts that serves as the foundation for any subsequent affections, but only the sudden and direct way in which the texts came to mind, the affections are not of a spiritual nature. "For, as has been shown, the sudden coming of the words to their minds, is no evidence that the bringing 'em to their minds in that manner, was from God. And if it was true that God brought the words to their minds, and they certainly knew it, that would not be spiritual knowledge; it may be without any spiritual sense." So "these affections which are built on that notion, that texts of Scripture are sent immediately from God, are built on no spiritual foundation, and are vain and delusive."

Let's suppose a person "hears" in his mind the words of Luke 12:32, that it is the Father's good pleasure to grant the kingdom to the followers of his Son. He rejoices and finds such words sweet and wonderful and excellent. "But the reason why the promise seems excellent to 'em, is only because they think it is made to them immediately. All the sense they have of any glory in them is only from self-love and from their own imagined interest in the words. [It isn't] that they had any view or sense of the holy and glorious nature of the kingdom of heaven, and the spiritual glory of that God who gives it, and of his excellent grace to sinful men in offering and giving them this kingdom, of his own good pleasure, preceding their imagined interest in these things, and their being affected by them, and being the foundation of their affection, and hope of an interest in them. On the contrary, they first imagine they are interested, and then are highly affected with that, and then can own these things to be excellent. So that the sudden and extraordinary way of the Scriptures coming to their mind, is plain[ly] the first foundation of the whole; which is a clear evidence of the wretched delusion they are under."

Far too many people find their comfort and assurance not in the beauty of the truth of Scripture but in what they perceive to be the immediate and sudden way in which the Spirit supposedly brings such truths to their minds. It is the *experience* of the revelation and not its *essence* in which they put their trust. Subsequently, their joy and confidence in life "is not anything contained in, or taught by these Scriptures, as they lie in the Bible, but the manner of their coming to them; which is a certain evidence of their delusion."

Is all this to say that the Spirit cannot or does not apply the promises of Scripture to our minds and hearts? Of course not. But we must note what that application is. "A spiritual application of the Word of God consists in applying it to the heart, in spiritually enlightening, sanctifying influences. A spiritual application of an invitation or offer of the gospel consists in giving the soul a spiritual sense or relish of the holy and divine blessings offered, and also the sweet and wonderful grace of the offerer, in making so gracious an offer, and of his holy excellency and faithfulness to fulfill what he offers, and his glorious sufficiency for it."

Thus a "spiritual application of the promises of Scripture, for the comfort of the saints, consists in enlightening their minds to see the holy excellency and sweetness of the blessings promised, and also the holy excellency of the promiser, and his faithfulness and sufficiency, thus drawing forth their hearts to embrace the promiser, and [the] thing promised."

An alleged application "not consisting in this divine sense and enlightening of the mind, but consisting only in the words being borne into the thoughts, as if immediately then spoken, so making persons believe, on no other foundation, that the promise is theirs, is a blind application, and belongs to the spirit of darkness, and not of light."

Many have claimed that they are the recipients of God's saving grace because "secret facts" have been immediately suggested to their minds. By "secret facts" we mean information that does not come from argumentation or reason or from any of the five senses. It is information that could not be gained by any means other than extraordinary suggestion. But this is no proof of God's saving presence, for there is nothing in the nature of these perceptions that is *divinely excellent* and beyond what people might know or learn eventually through the exercise of their normal faculties of sense and reason. If it were the Spirit producing these ideas in the minds of those who are truly saved "not only the manner of producing the effect, but the effect" itself would be "vastly above all that can be in an unsanctified [i.e., unsaved] mind."

There is nothing to prevent God from putting such "secret facts" in a person's mind by the exertion of his immediate power. But this does not mean the recipient of such facts is thereby saved. Indeed, "God can if he pleases, extraordinarily and immediately suggest this to, and impress it upon an unsanctified mind now."

Even the so-called "witness of the Spirit" that many claim to have experienced is not necessarily a sign of a supernatural and gracious activity of God. Being inwardly and immediately convinced that one is a child of God does not in itself prove that it is true. When the Spirit "bears witness with our spirit" that we are children of God (Rom. 8:16), he opens our eyes to see what has already been revealed in the Word and he enables us to conclude, based on evidence, that we are the children of God. This is not a reference to some immediate voice spoken directly to the mind of a person communicating the assurance that one is saved.

What I am objecting to here is the idea that one can gain full assurance of salvation based solely on the manner in which the assurance is allegedly imparted to the mind. If such assurance is impressed on the mind by some immediate disclosure and does not also entail evidence or signs of a transformed heart, the former is weak grounds for concluding that one is saved. The witness or seal of the Spirit is the actual work of grace in the soul that changes it to live in conformity with the commands of Scripture. Or again, "this earnest of the Spirit, and first fruits of the Spirit, which has been shown to be the same with the seal of the Spirit, is the vital, gracious, sanctifying communication and influence of the Spirit, and not any immediate suggestion or revelation of facts by the Spirit."

The Spirit bearing witness with our spirit that we are children of God is seen from the immediately preceding context to refer to his indwelling of us and leading us, as a spirit of adoption, to obey the Father's will. "So that it appears that the witness of the Spirit the Apostle speaks of is far from being any whisper or immediate suggestion or revelation; [rather, it is] that gracious holy effect of the Spirit of God in the hearts of the saints, the disposition and temper of children, appearing in sweet childlike love to God, which casts out fear, or a spirit of a slave."

THE SECOND SIGN OF AUTHENTIC AFFECTIONS

The first objective ground of gracious affections is the transcendently excellent and amiable nature of divine things as they are in themselves, and not any conceived relation they bear to self, or self-interest.

THE PRIMARY POINT OF this second sure sign of genuine religious affections is that "the divine excellency and glory of God, and Jesus Christ, the Word of God, the works of God, and the ways of God, etc., is the primary reason, why a true saint loves these things; and not any supposed interest that he has in them, or any conceived benefit that he has received from them, or shall receive from them, or any such imagined relation which they bear to his interest."

Perhaps the most common view is that a person is motivated by self-love to delight in the excellency of God. In other words, a person loves the glory of God because he is convinced that such will bring him joy and happiness. But why is he so convinced? What is it about beholding God's glory that leads him to regard it as the chief means to attain his own happiness? Surely there must have been some change or alteration in a person's mind and heart in which he apprehends a beauty and splendor in God's nature as it is in itself. This is what first draws a person to God and causes his heart to be united to him before he ever considers that it also will be a boon to his own happiness.

God is, in and of himself, lovely. God is, in and of himself, supremely sublime and excellent and worthy of being beheld and enjoyed as such. It is for the sake of that beauty and brightness and glory of God in himself that a true believer loves him.

This isn't to say that a person can't love God because of the favor and love that God shows him. Often people become aware of the reality of hell and how the grace of God in Christ has delivered them from it, and this becomes the first thing that evokes their affections of love and joy. Only after they are made aware that God has forgiven and accepted them in Christ do they acknowledge that he is lovely and excellent in himself.

But the experience of love in true Christians comes about in a different way. "They don't first see that God loves them and then see that he is lovely; but they first see that God is lovely and that Christ is excellent and glorious, and their hearts are first captivated with this view, and the exercises of their love are wont from time to time to begin here, and to arise primarily from these views; and then, consequentially, they see God's love and great favor to them." Thus their affection for God is because of what they see in God himself. Love for self and what happiness they may attain in this glorious God is secondary and consequential to their recognition of his intrinsic beauty.

When a Christian feels gratitude to God for his kindness and grace, it arises from a prior foundation of love for God for what he is in himself. "The saint having seen the glory of God, and his heart being overcome by it, and captivated into a supreme love to him on that account, his heart hereby becomes tender, and easily affected with kindnesses received." The saving grace of God in Christ and the glorious work of redemption is a thing intrinsically beautiful and marvelous and would be so whether or not we as individuals were ever the recipients of it.

But doesn't John say that we love God because God first loved us (see 1 John 4:19)? Yes, but his point is primarily that God loved us before we ever had any affection for him and that our love for him is therefore the fruit of his love for us. We love God because he has granted us the capacity to love him. Furthermore, the love God has for people who don't love him is itself one of the reasons why God is excellent and glorious and deserving of our praise. When one, by grace, recognizes that he or she is the object of such glorious love, love in return rises up in one's heart.

What is true about believers' love for God is also true of their joy and spiritual delight and pleasure. "The first foundation of it is not any consideration or conception of their interest in divine things; but it primarily consists in the sweet entertainment their minds have in the view or contemplation of the divine and holy beauty of these things, as they are in themselves." This is, in fact, what differentiates between the joy of the hypocrite and the joy of the true child of God. The former "rejoices in himself. Self is the first foundation of his joy. The latter rejoices in God. The hypocrite has his mind pleased and delighted, in the first place, with his own privilege and the happiness which he supposes he has attained or shall attain. True saints have their minds, in the first place, inexpressibly pleased and delighted with the sweet ideas of the glorious and amiable nature of the things of God. And this is the spring of all their delights, and the cream of all their pleasures. 'Tis the joy of their joy. This sweet and ravishing entertainment they have in the view of the beautiful and delightful nature of divine things is the foundation of the joy that they have afterwards, in the consideration of [those divine things] being theirs. But the dependence of the affections of hypocrites is in a contrary order: they first rejoice, and are elevated with it, that they are made so much of by God; and then on that ground, he seems in a sort, lovely to them."

Thus "the first foundation of the delight a true saint has in God, is his [i.e., God's] own perfection; and the first foundation of the delight he has in Christ, is his own beauty; he appears in himself the chief among ten thousand, and altogether lovely. The way of salvation by Christ is a delightful way to him, for the sweet and admirable manifestations of the divine perfections in it. The holy doctrines of the gospel by which God is exalted and man abased, holiness honored and promoted, and sin greatly disgraced and discouraged, and free and sovereign love manifested, are glorious doctrines in his eyes, and sweet to his taste, prior to any conception of his interest in these things. Indeed the saints rejoice in their interest in God, and that Christ is theirs, and so they have great reason; but this is not the first spring of their joy. They first rejoice in God as glorious and excellent in himself, and then secondarily rejoice in it that so glorious a God is theirs. They first have their hearts filled with sweetness from the view of Christ's excellency, and the excellency of his grace, and the beauty of the way of salvation

by him; and then they have a secondary joy, in that so excellent a Savior
and such excellent grace is theirs."

We must, therefore, be careful that our primary joy is in God, as
he is in and of himself, and not in our experience of God. That we have
been made recipients of his grace and are enabled to behold his beauty
is a marvelous thing indeed. But it is secondary and consequential to
a recognition of God's inherent excellency. What brings you greatest
and most immediate delight: *your experience* of a revelation of Christ,
or *Christ* revealed?

A true child of God, "when in the enjoyment of true discoveries of
the sweet glory of God and Christ has his mind too much captivated
and engaged by what he views without [i.e., external to] himself, to
stand at that time to view himself, and his own attainments. It would
be a diversion and loss which he could not bear, to take his eye off from
the ravishing object of his contemplation to survey his own experience,
and to spend time in thinking with himself, what an high attainment
this is, and what a good story I now have to tell others. Nor does the
pleasure and sweetness of his mind at that time chiefly arise from the
consideration of the safety of his state, or anything he has in view of his
own qualifications, experiences, or circumstances; but from the divine
and supreme beauty of what is the object of his direct view, without
himself; which sweetly entertains and strongly holds his mind."[1]

---

[1]This statement raises the question, could Jonathan Edwards be called a "Christian hedonist," to
borrow John Piper's terminology? For an excellent answer in the affirmative to that question, see
Piper's article, "Was Jonathan Edwards a Christian Hedonist?" at www.desiringgod.org.

10

THE THIRD SIGN OF AUTHENTIC AFFECTIONS

Those affections that are truly holy, are primarily founded on the loveliness of the moral excellency of divine things. Or (to express it otherwise), a love for divine things for the beauty and sweetness of their moral excellency is the first beginning and spring of all holy affections.

IN USING THE WORD *moral* to define the excellency of divine things we are not speaking of adherence to some objective standard of behavior. Rather, by the moral perfections of God we mean "those attributes which God exercises as a moral agent, or whereby the heart and will of God are good, right, and infinitely becoming, and lovely, such as his righteousness, truth, faithfulness, and goodness; or, in one word, his holiness." By God's natural attributes or perfections we mean "those attributes, wherein, according to our way of conceiving of God, consists, not the holiness or moral goodness of God, but his greatness, such as his power, his knowledge whereby he knows all things, and his being eternal, from everlasting to everlasting, his omnipresence, and his awful and terrible majesty."

As noted, we can reduce our description of the moral excellency of God to his holiness. Holiness is that word in Scripture which encompasses God's "purity and beauty as a moral agent, comprehending all his moral perfections, his righteousness, faithfulness and goodness."

In our discussion of the second sign of authentic affections, we noted that the first ground of all holy affections is the supreme excellency of divine things as they are in themselves. We now can say that the "kind of excellency of the nature of divine things, which is the first objective ground of all holy affections, is their moral excellency or their holiness."

Therefore, the love that true saints have for God is for the beauty of his holiness or his moral perfection as being supremely lovely in itself. Certainly we love God for all his attributes. They are each amiable and lovely in themselves. Contemplating each and every one of the divine perfections is exceedingly and indescribably pleasant. But when it comes to the regenerate, "their love to God for his holiness is what is most fundamental and essential in their love. . . . A love to God for the beauty of his moral attributes, leads to and necessarily causes a delight in God for all his attributes."

If a being were merely strong but not holy, there would be no loveliness in it. If a being were merely knowledgeable but not holy, there would be little of intrinsic worth to call forth our praise. God's wisdom is glorious because it is holy. God's immutability is glorious because it is a holy immutability and not "an inflexible obstinacy in wickedness." Thus a true love for God must begin with "a delight in his holiness, and not with a delight in any other attribute, for no other attribute is truly lovely without this."

The same is true of all divine things. The people of God are beautiful because they are, by grace, holy ones (i.e., saints). Angels are beautiful because they are holy, rather than being evil (like the demons). The Christian religion surpasses all others because it is holy. The excellency of the Scriptures is found in their holiness.

"Herein does primarily consist the amiableness and beauty of the Lord Jesus, whereby he is the chief among ten thousands and altogether lovely." Indeed, "all the spiritual beauty of his human nature, consisting in his meekness, lowliness, patience, heavenliness, love to God, love to men, condescension to the mean and vile, and compassion to the miserable, etc., is all summed up in his holiness. And the beauty of his divine nature, of which the beauty of his human nature is the image and reflection, does also primarily consist in his holiness." The gospel is glorious because it is a holy gospel. And "herein chiefly consists the glory of heaven, that it is the holy city, the holy Jerusalem, the habitation of God's holiness, and so of his glory (Isa. 63:15)."

In our discussion of the first sign of genuine affections we note that God grants to the regenerate a new supernatural sense that is unattainable by use of any of the normal five senses of the body. We can now proceed to say that it is *the beauty of holiness* which is "that thing in spiritual and divine things, which is perceived by this spiritual sense, that is so diverse from all that natural men perceive in them. This kind of beauty is the quality that is the immediate object of this spiritual sense. This is the sweetness that is the proper object of this spiritual taste."

In Psalm 119 the law of God is described as the "grand expression and emanation of the holiness of God's nature." It is repeatedly portrayed as "the food and entertainment, and as the great object of the love, the appetite, the complacence and rejoicing of the gracious nature, which prizes God's commandments above gold, yea, the finest gold, and to which they are sweeter than the honey, and honeycomb; and that upon account of their holiness."

In heaven, it is the holiness of God that primarily engages the worship and adoration of the angels and saints (see Isa. 6:3; Rev. 4:8; 15:4). So, too, the saints on earth do worship and praise God for his holiness above all else (see Ps. 98:1; 99:2–3, 5, 8–9; 97:11–12).

This is the way by which true saints may be distinguished from merely natural, unsaved, men. The unregenerate "have no sense of the goodness and excellency of holy things, at least for their holiness. They have no taste of that kind of good." But the regenerate "by the mighty power of God, have it discovered [i.e., revealed] to them. They have that supernatural, most noble and divine sense given them, by which they perceive it, and it is this that captivates their hearts, and delights them above all things. 'Tis the most amiable and sweet thing to the heart of a true saint, that is to be found in heaven or earth, that which above all others attracts and engages his soul, and that wherein, above all things, he places his happiness, and which he lots [i.e., rests or relies] upon for solace and entertainment to his mind, in this world, and full satisfaction and blessedness in another."

By this you may examine the state of your own soul and the quality of your love to God and Jesus and his Word, as well as your love for God's people and your desire for heaven: do you love them all "from a supreme delight in this sort of beauty, without being primarily moved from your imagined interest in them, or expectations from 'em."

A person can be greatly moved by the natural perfections of God and not be saved. A person can be stirred with admiration for God's power and greatness "and yet be entirely blind to the beauty of his moral perfection, and have nothing of that spiritual taste which relishes this divine sweetness." Even Satan and his demons know God in this way, yet they are utterly destitute of any sense or relish of that kind of divine beauty which consists in his moral perfections or holiness.

When God finally brings all into judgment, those who are cast into hell will see everything of God except the beauty of his holiness. They will see and know his power and wisdom and knowledge and strength and greatness and majesty and eternity and immutability and justice and righteousness, but they will find or sense or see or relish no beauty in them.

But the regenerate see the beauty and glory and relish the sweetness of all such divine perfections. Indeed, this is what "will melt and humble the hearts of men, and wean them from the world, and draw them to God, and effectually change them. A sight of the awful greatness of God may overpower men's strength, and be more than they can endure. But if the moral beauty of God be hid, the enmity of the heart will remain in its full strength, no love will be enkindled, all will not be effectual to gain the will, but that will remain inflexible, whereas the first glimpse of the moral and spiritual glory of God shining into the heart, produces all these effects, as it were with omnipotent power, which nothing can withstand."

It really matters little, therefore, if people speak of what they perceive as great revelations of divine power and greatness, but never taste or sense or relish the sweetness and loveliness and glory of God.

11

THE FOURTH SIGN OF AUTHENTIC AFFECTIONS

Gracious affections do arise from the mind's being enlightened, rightly and spiritually to understand or apprehend divine things.

HOLY AND AUTHENTIC affections are always the fruit or effect of some spiritual instruction or understanding of the mind. The mind is certainly capable of being affected with things other than knowledge or instruction. People can perceive some new shape or shining light or beautiful object and be profoundly moved and stirred by what they experience. But if the "idea" or sense does not entail knowledge of God or new insights into the perfections of his nature and works, the affections it produces are of no benefit.

All true and gracious affections arise from some enlightenment of the mind in which a person is taught about God and Christ. It might be a new perspective on the spiritual excellencies of Jesus or the glory of that salvation he has graciously obtained for us. "Such enlightenings of the understanding as these, are things entirely different in their nature, from strong ideas of shapes and colors, and outward brightness and glory, or sounds and voices."

As we noted earlier, some claim that their affections are from God because they were aroused by the experience of Scripture texts spontaneously coming to mind. But if the mind is not enlightened by the *content* of those texts—that is to say, if there is no understanding derived from the truth they embody—the affections that result are useless. When the disciples spoke to Jesus on the road to Emmaus, they made it clear that their affections were the result of a new *understanding* of Scripture (Luke 24:32).

Nor are those affections genuine which arise from a misunderstanding of some text of the Bible or an alleged insight that is unrelated to the context and intent of the original author. Nor are those affections genuine which are grounded in some physical sensation in the body. People often experience exhilaration or some pleasant sensation in the body, from which certain affections arise.

That spiritual understanding or intellectual sense from which genuine affections arise is peculiar to the true people of God. See, for example, 1 Corinthians 2:14; 1 John 3:6; 3 John 11; John 6:40; Matthew 11:27; John 12:45; and Colossians 1:9. This spiritual understanding "consists in the sensations of a new spiritual sense, which the souls of natural men have not." The immediate object of this sense, as noted earlier, is the supreme beauty and excellency of the nature of divine things as they are in themselves.

This knowledge of the loveliness and intrinsic excellency of divine things is the essence of true religion. Spiritual understanding, then, "consists in a sense of the heart of the supreme beauty and sweetness of the holiness or moral perfection of divine things, together with all that discerning and knowledge of things of religion, that depends upon, and flows from such a sense."

This is a *sense* of the heart, and not mere speculative or theoretical knowledge. In other words, "there is a distinction to be made between a mere notional understanding, wherein the mind only beholds things in the exercise of a speculative faculty; and the sense of the heart, wherein the mind don't only speculate and behold, but relishes and feels. That sort of knowledge by which a man has a sensible perception of amiableness and loathsomeness, or of sweetness and nauseousness, is not just the same sort of knowledge with that by which he knows what a triangle is and what a square is. The one is mere speculative knowledge; the other sensible knowledge, in which more than the mere intellect is concerned; the heart is the proper subject of it, or the soul as a being that not only beholds, but has inclination, and is pleased or displeased. And yet there is the nature of instruction in it; as he that has perceived the sweet taste of honey, knows much more about it than he who has only looked upon and felt of it."

Thus a saving or spiritual understanding consists primarily in this sense or taste of the moral beauty of divine things. When this sense is revealed to the human soul, it enables a person to see the glory of all God's perfections and work of redemption in Christ. One more fully understands the sufficiency of Christ as mediator once the beauty of his moral perfections is revealed. When saints see Christ's moral beauty they become joyously aware of the preciousness of his blood and its capacity to save. Indeed, when the soul beholds the moral beauty of the person of Christ, one sees the glory of the way of salvation, the glory of the Word of God, and even the true evil of sin, "for he who sees the beauty of holiness, must necessarily see the hatefulness of sin, its contrary."

And "he that sees the beauty of holiness, or true moral good, sees the greatest and most important thing in the world, which is the fullness of all things, without which all the world is empty, no better than nothing, yea, worse than nothing. Unless this is seen, nothing is seen that is worth the seeing, for there is no other true excellency or beauty."

The unsaved are also the object of the Spirit's influence when it comes to an understanding of the things of God. Unregenerate people are able, with God's assistance, to see the truth of the gospel and the goodness of what God has done for sinners in Christ Jesus. However, their understanding never progresses beyond that point. The saved, on the other hand, don't merely understand the principles of the gospel, they *relish* them. They don't merely see the truth of what Christ has done for sinners, they *savor* it. They perceive in the gospel the holy beauty of divine things and have a sense of the sweetness of what God has accomplished in Christ.

But we must also point out that this new sense or spiritual understanding that is graciously granted the regenerate is *not new doctrinal knowledge*. It is not as if God reveals theological truths and propositions never before heard or seen or written in Scripture. What the Spirit awakens in the soul is a *new taste* or *relish of the beauty and sweetness* of the propositions that the mind has already come to know.

The Spirit doesn't provide "any new doctrinal explanation of any part of the Scripture," nor does this work consist "in opening to the mind the mystical meaning of the Scripture." In fact, it is entirely possible "that a man might know how to interpret all the types, parables, enigmas, and allegories in the Bible, and not have one beam of spiritual light in his mind; because he may not have the least degree of that spiritual sense of the holy beauty of divine things which has been spoken of, and may see nothing of this kind of glory in anything contained in any of these mysteries, or any other part of the Scripture."

This spiritual understanding or new sense imparted to the regenerate does not consist of an individual learning God's will for his or her life. To gain that sort of knowledge is no different from learning a new doctrinal proposition about the nature or work of God. For example, let's imagine a person struggling with whether he is to venture into a dangerous land to preach the gospel. He prays, asking God to reveal his perfect will. Suddenly he has impressed on his heart the words God spoke to Jacob in Genesis 46, "Fear not to go down into Egypt; . . . I will go down with thee . . . ; and I will also surely bring thee up again" (vv. 3-4, KJV). Although those words applied specifically to Jacob, the person feels that God has a further meaning in them that indicates he is to undertake this missionary journey and that God will bring him safely home. To suggest that a new meaning has emerged from Scripture "is the same thing as making a new Scripture; it is . . . adding to the word," something which warrants the curse of God.

Rather, to spiritually understand the Bible "is to have the eyes of the mind opened, to behold the wonderful spiritual excellency of the glorious things contained in the true meaning of it, and that always were contained in it, ever since it was written; to behold the amiable and bright manifestations of the divine perfections, and of the excellency and sufficiency of Christ, and the excellency and suitableness of the way of salvation by Christ, and the spiritual glory of the precepts and promises of the Scripture."

What people typically refer to as the "leading" of the Holy Spirit consists primarily in instructing someone what his duty is to perform and inducing him to comply with that instruction. But this "instruction" consists "in a person's being guided by a spiritual and distinguishing taste of that which has in it true moral beauty." In other words, the person is awakened to whether an action is right or wrong by being enlightened to see and taste and sense its intrinsic moral beauty or intrinsic moral deformity. This also demonstrates the difference between what we have called "spiritual understanding" and those many experiences in which people claim to have "seen" Christ and heaven; have had God's love spoken directly into their hearts; have had impressions of what the future holds; have had immediate revelations of secret facts; have had Scripture texts brought to mind that are applied in ways beyond their original intent; or have experienced what they believe are interpretations of the mystical meaning of the Bible.

12

THE FIFTH SIGN OF AUTHENTIC AFFECTIONS

Truly gracious affections are attended with a reasonable and spiritual conviction of the judgment, of the reality and certainty of divine things.

ALL WHO ARE REGENERATED by the Spirit have a solid and thorough conviction of the truth of the glory of the gospel. All arguments are silenced. All doubting is cast aside. So assured are they of the reality of gospel truths "that they are not afraid to venture their all upon their truth."

This conviction in believers' souls is effectual, which is to say it exerts an influence on their hearts and thereby governs and rules their affections. They perceive the reality of God's revelation in Jesus Christ with such clarity that it exerts life-changing power on their hearts and their behavior. So powerful is this influence that in the absence of a change in ethical conduct, one may conclude that saving knowledge of the gospel is absent. Numerous biblical texts bear witness to this sort of effectual conviction and persuasion of the truth in the hearts of God's people, such as Matthew 16:15–17; John 6:68–69; 17:6–8; Acts 8:37; 2 Corinthians 4:11–18; 2 Timothy 1:12; Hebrews 3:6; 11:1; and 1 John 4:13–16; 5:4–5.

Some people are persuaded they are saved because they have had biblical texts spontaneously come to mind, from which they deduce that they are the objects of God's saving love and have had their sins forgiven. But as we've already seen, and will note in more depth later on, "there is no Scripture which declares that any person is in a good estate directly, or any other way than by consequence." "Consequence" means the fruit of a transformed life, consisting of tangible evidence of a progressive conformity to the mind and will of God.

This persuasion or conviction of the truth of the gospel, if it is redemptive, must be reasonable. In other words, it must be established "on real evidence, or upon that which is a good reason, or just ground of conviction." Merely believing the gospel because one heard it from parents or read about it during the course of one's education is insufficient. A conviction concerning the truth of the gospel must be spiritual in nature. Judas Iscariot "believed" Jesus to be the Messiah, but was clearly unregenerate. The crowd in John 2:23–25 who "believed" in Jesus' name upon seeing his miracles were yet in unbelief, as was Simon Magus in Acts 8:13, 23.

The belief or conviction of the redeemed is of a different quality from that which the unregenerate experience (see John 17:8; Titus 1:1; John 16:27; 1 John 4:15; 5:1, 19). A *spiritual* conviction of the truth of the gospel, as we noted earlier, "is such a conviction, as arises from having a spiritual view or apprehension of those things in the mind." True faith always arises from a *spiritual sight* of Christ (see Luke 10:21–22; John 6:40; 17:6–8; Matt. 16:16–17). This "sight" consists of a new "sense and taste of the divine, supreme and holy excellency and beauty of those things" of the gospel.

This view or sense of the glory and unparalleled beauty of the things of the gospel persuades our minds in two ways:

(1) In the first case, the glory of the gospel may be imparted to the mind by a direct and supernatural act of God such that the glory is itself the proof of its divinity. A person knows it to be true *intuitively*, not by being persuaded on other grounds to believe the reality of what is revealed. They simply see it in its glory and know it to be of God. This isn't to say that a person comes to this conviction "without any argument or deduction at all, but it is without any long chain of arguments. The argument is but one, and the evidence direct. The mind ascends to the truth of the gospel but by one step, and that is its divine glory."

There is such a transcendent and glorious quality inherent in the things of the gospel that, unlike other, merely human truths, they convince and satisfy on the basis of their own intrinsic and ineffable excellency. This is to say that "the manifestations of the moral and spiritual glory of the divine Being (which is the proper beauty of the Divinity) bring their own evidence, and tend to assure the heart" (see 2 Pet. 1:16–18).

If there are ineffable, altogether unique, excellencies in the gospel, it makes sense that they can be discerned by "the special influence and enlightenings of the Spirit of God." If one needs special skills and insights to understand a great literary genius such as Milton or Shakespeare, how much more is such required to discern the truths in a book written by God! When we factor in human depravity and the dullness of heart and mind that it engenders, it seems evident that men will not see the glories of the gospel unless "God is pleased to enlighten them, and restore an holy taste, to discern and relish divine beauties."

Once the truth of the gospel is, by this divine and supernatural light, made known to the mind, all sorts of other biblical truths are seen. For example, once one is persuaded of the glory of the gospel, he sees the exceeding evil of sin, "for the same eye that discerns the transcendent beauty of holiness, necessarily therein sees the exceeding odiousness of sin, [and] the same taste which relishes the sweetness of true moral good, tastes the bitterness of moral evil. And by this means a man sees his own sinfulness and loathsomeness, for he has now a sense to discern objects of this nature, and so sees the truth of what the Word of God declares concerning the exceeding sinfulness of mankind, which before he did not see." Indeed, one can see the whole of the biblical revelation, for once a sense of true divine beauty is imparted to the soul, the believer discerns the beauty of every part of the gospel scheme.

Apart from this direct apprehension of the intrinsic glory of the gospel, people may acknowledge that the gospel is "probably" true and that it appears "rational." But "to have a conviction, so clear and evident and assuring, as to be sufficient to induce them, with boldness, to sell all, confidently and fearlessly to run the venture of the loss of all things, and of enduring the most exquisite and long-continued torments, and to trample the world under foot, and count all things but dung, for Christ; the evidence they can have from history cannot be sufficient." No matter how extensive their learning or how probable their proofs, many will still have doubts and concerns and anxieties about the gospel's truthfulness.

And what about those who have little, if any, education? If a clear conviction of the truth of Christianity must await their education, propagating the gospel in their midst will be infinitely difficult.

Clearly, God has made it possible for a person to attain full assurance of the truth of the gospel apart from arguments related to ancient traditions and history and other evidences. Perhaps most of those in the history of the church came to a solid and saving faith apart from intricate historical and logical arguments. Those who eventually lost their lives as martyrs of Christ, perhaps most of whom lacked formal education, "declare their assurance of the truth and divinity of the gospel, having had the eyes of their minds enlightened, to see divinity in the gospel, or to behold that unparalleled, ineffably excellent, and truly divine glory shining in it, which is altogether distinguishing, evidential, and convincing, so that they may truly be said to have seen God in it, and to have seen that it is indeed divine."

We are not to disparage or wholly exclude any role for external evidences of the truth of the gospel. Often such arguments can awaken unbelievers to serious consideration of the gospel or they may serve to confirm and reassure the faith of those who are true saints. But the fact remains that "there is no spiritual conviction of the judgment, but what arises from an apprehension of the spiritual beauty and glory of divine things."

(2) As noted above, there are two ways in which the divine glory convinces the mind of the truth of Christianity. We have just explored how this occurs directly. We will now examine two ways in which it does so indirectly.

First, the divine and supernatural light imparted to the soul of a person removes those prejudices of the heart against the truth, "so that the mind thereby lies open to the force of the reasons which are offered." The fallen mind is at enmity with the gospel and is naturally hostile to the things of Christ. But when God reveals the glory of the gospel to a person, it "destroys that enmity, and removes the prejudices, and sanctifies the reason, and causes it to be open and free."

Why is it, for example, that the miracles of Jesus had a vastly different effect on the minds of the disciples than they did on the minds of the Scribes and Pharisees? Clearly it was because, in the case of the former, "their reason was sanctified, and those blinding prejudices, which the Scribes and Pharisees were under, were removed, by the sense they had of the excellency of Christ and his doctrine."

Second, this divine light "not only removes the hindrances of reason, but positively helps reason. It makes even the speculative notions more lively. It assists and engages the attention of the mind" to consider the truths of the gospel. The concepts presented in the gospel, which otherwise may appear dim and obscure, "by this means have a light cast upon them, and are impressed with greater strength, so that the mind can better judge of them."

We mustn't forget, however, that there is a degree of conviction concerning the truth of the gospel that arises "from the common enlightenings of the Spirit of God." This is what theologians have traditionally meant when they spoke of the "common grace" of God. The Spirit can awaken in people a measure of conviction concerning the reality of their sin and the natural perfections of God and the overall truthfulness of Scripture without necessarily regenerating their hearts. "These things persons may have, and yet have no sense of the beauty and amiableness of the moral and holy excellency that is in the things of religion, and therefore no spiritual conviction of their truth. But yet such convictions are sometimes mistaken for saving convictions, and the affections flowing from 'em, for saving affections."

Oftentimes, "the extraordinary impressions which are made on the imaginations of some persons, in the visions, and immediate strong impulses and suggestions that they have, as though they saw sights, and had words spoken to 'em, may, and often do beget a strong persuasion of the truth of invisible things." But in the long run, such experiences serve only to lead people away from the Word of God and into fanaticism. Satan is certainly capable of misleading people in this way, thus leading them into a false assurance of salvation.

13

THE SIXTH SIGN OF AUTHENTIC AFFECTIONS

Gracious affections are attended with evangelical humiliation.

TRUE, GODLY HUMILITY IS "a sense that a Christian has of his own utter insufficiency, despicableness, and odiousness, with an answerable frame of heart."

Unregenerate people can feel a lowliness or smallness or natural humility when they are made aware of the greatness of God and their failure to honor him. But "they don't see their own odiousness on the account of sin; they don't see the hateful nature of sin. A sense of this is given in evangelical humiliation, by a discovery of the beauty of God's holiness and moral perfection." If there is genuine humility, there will be "an answerable frame of heart, consisting in a disposition to abase themselves and exalt God alone."

There is nothing more essential to the presence of saving grace in the soul than humility. Those who lack humility most assuredly lack saving grace (see, e.g., Ps. 34:18; 51:17; 138:6; Prov. 3:34; Isa. 57:15; 66:1–2; Mic. 6:8; Matt. 5:3; 18:3–4).

Humility is one of the two essential elements in self-denial. In the first element, a person denies and resists his sinful and worldly inclinations and labors in the grace of God to renounce and avoid wicked activities. In the second element, he denies and resists the tendency of his heart toward self-exaltation and self-promotion and praise.

Hypocrites are quite good at making much of their humility and speaking lowly of themselves and their attainments. Such folk loudly proclaim their lowliness and then expect others to praise them for it! They are quick to make known their failures and their humility but react with strong protest if someone in private should suggest that their claims to humility are feigned and superficial.

The fact is that "some who think themselves quite emptied of themselves, and are confident that they are abased in the dust, are full as they can hold with the glory of their own humility, and lifted up to heaven with an high opinion of their own abasement. Their humility is a swelling, self-conceited, confident, showy, noisy, assuming humility. It seems to be the nature of spiritual pride to make men conceited and ostentatious of their humility."

Although this sort of spiritual pride is insidious and often secret, there are at least two ways it shows itself:

(1) First, the person who is in the grip of spiritual pride is more likely to think highly of his attainments in religion when he compares himself with others. He is like the Pharisee who prayed, "God, I thank you that I am not like other men" (Luke 18:11). This is often manifested by how quick he is to assume the role of leader. He sees himself as uniquely qualified to teach and guide and direct and manage. He expects others to regard him as such and to yield to his authority in matters of faith.

The person of true humility, on the other hand, "is apt to think his attainments in religion to be comparatively mean and to esteem himself low among the saints, and one of the least of saints. Humility, or true lowliness of mind, disposes persons to think others better than themselves." They are disposed to think others are eminently more qualified to teach and to lead. They posture themselves to hear and to learn rather than to speak and to instruct. When they do speak, it feels unnatural to do so boldly and with a masterful tone, for "humility disposes 'em rather to speak trembling."

Those who are filled with spiritual pride speak often of what they perceive to be the extraordinary nature of their religious experiences. This isn't to say that our experiences of divine mercy are anything less than wonderful and glorious. But if one is inclined to think his experiences are great in comparison with those of others or beyond what is ordinarily the experience of the average saint, together with the expectation that others should admire and respect him for them, pride is assuredly at work. Of course, those lacking true humility don't regard their words as boasting or an expression of pride. After all, these are experiences of *divine* grace and mercy. These are things that God has done for them. But this was precisely the attitude of that Pharisee in Luke 18. He actually gives God the glory for making him different from others, whom he regards as beneath himself! "God, I thank you!" "Their verbally ascribing it to the grace of God, that they are holier than other saints, don't hinder their forwardness to think so highly of their holiness, being a sure evidence of the pride and vanity of their minds. If they were under the influence of an humble spirit, their attainments in religion would not be so apt to shine in their own eyes, nor would they be so much in admiring their own beauty."

Those Christians who are truly most eminent and have experienced extraordinary effusions of divine grace humble themselves as little children (Matt. 18:4). They are actually more astonished at their low degree of love and their ingratitude than they are by the heights of spiritual attainment and their knowledge of God.

"Such is the nature of grace, and of true spiritual light, that they naturally dispose the saints in the present state to look upon their grace and goodness little, and their deformity great." The truly humble soul is devastated by the smallest expression of depravity but nearly oblivious to great progress in goodness and obedience.

"That grace and holiness is worthy to be called little, that is, little in comparison of what it ought to be." The truly humble soul is always looking not at what he has attained, even if it be by divine grace, but at the rule or standard or goal for which his soul is striving. It is the latter by which he estimates and judges what he does and what he has accomplished. Therefore he will always regard his holiness and maturity as small because he compares it not with what others have attained, but with what is his own infinite obligation to attain.

God's grace in us opens our eyes to the reason why we should be holy. Thus, he who has more grace has a greater sense of the infinite excellency and glory of God and of the infinite dignity of Christ and the boundless length and breadth and depth and height of the love of Christ for sinners. This vision of God's infinite excellency only expands and grows with the increase of grace in the soul, to such an extent that one is increasingly astonished at the measure of his duty to love and honor this God. "And so the more he apprehends, the more the smallness of his grace and love appears strange and wonderful, and therefore is more ready to think that others are beyond him." *What stuns his soul is not that he loves God much but that one who is truly a child of God does not love God more.* This humble soul is likely to think such a reality unique to himself, for he sees only the outside of other Christians but the inside of himself.

Someone might object by saying that love for God increases in proportion to our knowledge of God, so how can this person's growth in knowing God lead him to regard his love for God as less, rather than more?

When a believer discovers something of God, he is made immediately aware of something far more in God that he had not heretofore seen. In other words, "there is something that is seen, that is wonderful; and that sight brings with it a strong conviction of something vastly beyond, that is not immediately seen. So that the soul, at the same time, is astonished at its ignorance, and that it knows so little, as well as that it loves so little."

When we grow in our knowledge of something that is finite, we feel that in a sense we have conquered it or subdued it and that we now control it because we have knowledge of it in all respects. But if the object of knowledge is infinite, as God is, with every measure of knowledge we attain we are made aware not of what we now know but of the incomparable degree of what we don't know. Allow me to quantify this point: assume that an object of knowledge tallies up to one hundred. As we gradually learn more about it, we gain seventy-five then eighty-five then ninety-five then ninety-nine and finally one hundred percent insight into what it is. But with something that is infinite, an increase of fifty percent of our knowledge in comparison with what we previously knew does not count for increase, because the object about which we are learning cannot be quantified or measured or ever ultimately attained.

Also, as we grow in our understanding of how infinite God is, we are ever more made aware of what our souls would know if only our ignorance were removed. This causes the soul "to complain greatly of spiritual ignorance and want of love, and long and reach after more knowledge and more love."

The highest love and knowledge of God we might attain in this world are not worthy to be compared with the *obligation* to love and know him once we consider the revelation of his infinite glory in his Word and works and in the gospel of Christ. And in comparison with the capacity God has given us to know him, what we do know of him appears small and trivial.

Therefore, "he that has much grace, apprehends much more than others that great height to which his love ought to ascend; and he sees better than others how little a way he has risen towards that height." This apprehension also reveals to him the depth and extent of his remaining corruption. "In order to judge how much corruption or sin we have remaining in us, we must take our measure from that height to which the rule of our duty extends."

The principle here is that with the increase of our knowledge of God comes an increase in our knowledge of our sin and how vast is the discrepancy between what we know and what we ought to know, between what we love and ought to love.

This also causes us to see that the smallest degree of ugliness in the least of all sins is greater than or outweighs the highest degree of beauty in the greatest of all holiness. "For the least sin against an infinite God, has an infinite hatefulness or deformity in it, but the highest degree of holiness in a creature has not an infinite loveliness in it. Therefore the loveliness of it is as nothing in comparison with the deformity of the least sin."

Since our obligation to God is infinite, the least failure to fulfill it (i.e., the least sin or failure to perform our duty) is infinitely ugly. This is because "our obligation to love and honor any being is in some proportion to his loveliness and honorableness, or to his worthiness to be loved and honored by us." In other words, "we are surely under greater obligation to love a more lovely being, than a less lovely: and if a Being be infinitely lovely or worthy to be loved by us, then our obligations to love him are infinitely great; and therefore, whatever is contrary to this love has in it infinite iniquity, deformity and unworthiness."

The point is that, contrary to the objection, as we grow in grace and knowledge and love of God, we continue to see more of our corruption and failure to properly honor God than we do of our love for him and our success in worshiping him.

If one's religious affections in any way or to any degree incline one to think that his sins are gone or that he is free from evil, this is a sure sign that the alleged "revelation" he has experienced is false. When God makes himself known to the soul, it is true that it serves to help restrain our sins. But it also and equally brings to light the extent of our corruption and depravity, disclosing to us our lack of humility and love and gratitude.

None of this is to deny that a person may know when he is the recipient of much divine grace. "But he won't be apt to know it; it won't be a thing obvious to him," that he has advanced beyond others in spiritual growth. In fact, "he must take pains to convince himself of it." Even then "it will hardly seem real to him, that he has more grace than they." Therefore, if a person easily persuades himself that he is, compared with others, an eminent and blessed saint, one who has experienced greater and more extraordinary things than others, he is certainly mistaken. He is, in fact, "under the great prevailings of a proud and self-righteous spirit." And if this turns out to be a habitual thing that is the prevailing temper of his mind, it indicates that he is not and never was a true believer in the first place.

Furthermore, experiences that have the tendency to elicit such self-evaluation are themselves vain and delusive. "Those supposed discoveries that naturally blow up the person with an admiration of the eminency of his discoveries, and fill him with conceit, that now he has seen and knows more than most other Christians, have nothing of the nature of true spiritual light in them. All true spiritual knowledge is of that nature, that the more a person has of it, the more is he sensible of his own ignorance."

(2) Second, another sign of spiritual pride is when a person is inclined to think highly of his humility. False religious affections have the tendency, especially when they are raised high and are intense, to make a person think that his humility is great.

But truly spiritual affections have the opposite effect. They actually lead a person to regard his present humility as small and insignificant and his present pride as great and exceedingly abominable.

This is true because a person typically measures his or her own humility by how much dignity they possess or the stature of their social standing. For example, if a powerful king should stoop to wash the feet of another powerful king who is his equal, he would regard it as an act of humility because of his own kingly stature. But if a poor slave should wash the feet of a great king, no one would take note of it or regard it as an act of humility.

"And the matter is no less plain and certain when worthless, vile and loathsome worms of the dust are apt to put such a construction on their acts of abasement before God, and to think it a token of great humility in them that they, under their affections, can find themselves so willing to acknowledge themselves to be so mean and unworthy, and to behave themselves as those that are so inferior. The very reason why such outward acts, and such inward exercises, look like great abasement in such an one is because he has a high conceit of himself."

On the other hand, if he thought more accurately of himself and considered his place in life, he would be stunned by his pride and wonder why he was not brought even lower before God. If you ever find yourself saying, "This act of devotion or love or service is certainly characterized by great humility," you obviously are in the grip of great pride, for you have an unduly and sinfully exalted view of your place vis-à-vis God. One thinks himself high and looks at his actions in comparison with his stature and thus regards it as truly humble that he should have performed such a service.

But in the truly humble soul, it is the opposite. A truly humble person knows his lowliness and sinfulness and thus, "when he is brought lowest of all, it does not appear to him that he is brought below his proper station, but that he is not come to it. He appears to himself yet vastly above it. He longs to get lower, that he may come to it, but appears at a great distance from it. And this distance he calls pride. And therefore his pride appears great to him, and not his humility. For although he is brought much lower than he used to be, yet it don't appear to him worthy of the name of humiliation, for him that is so infinitely mean and detestable to come down to a place which, though it be lower than what he used to assume, is yet vastly higher than what is proper for him."

In other words, the truly humble person will *never* consider an act to be *beneath his dignity*. Even if the act brings him lower than he has ever experienced before, he will always regard it as higher than he deserves.

The truly humble person never thinks his humility is great, because he has a proper grasp of the cause of his humility. Knowing the cause to be infinite, his abasement and lowliness can never be too great. "The cause why he should be abased appears so great, and the abasement of the frame of his heart so greatly short of it, that he takes much more notice of his pride than [of] his humility."

Or to put it yet another way, the person who is greatly under the conviction for sin is not inclined to think that he is greatly convicted. The truly humble person attributes his conviction to the greatness of the *cause* of his conviction, not to his own sensibility of sin. "That man is under great convictions whose conviction is great in proportion to his sin. But no man that is truly under great convictions thinks his conviction great in proportion to his sin. For if he does, 'tis a certain sign that he inwardly thinks his sins small. And if that be the case, that is a certain evidence that his conviction is small." And this, by the way, is the primary reason why people, when under a work of humiliation, are not sensible of it.

The truly humble person never thinks his sensibility of his own lowliness and filthiness is great, because he has a grasp of the cause of why he should be sensible of his sin. Knowing the infinite nature of divine glory and grace, the humble person is less likely to be aware of his humility than anything else in his soul! The greatest sense he has is of his pride, and wonders why he does not experience a greater humility than he does. On the other hand, "the deluded hypocrite, that is under the power of spiritual pride, is so blind to nothing as his pride; and so quicksighted to nothing as the shows of humility that are in him."

The humble believer is more apt to find fault with his own pride than with that of others. But the prideful man is quick to see the pride in others and not at all in himself.

The truly humble are not inclined to talk about their humility or to display it by means of eloquence or in any manner of living. True humility is not noisy, especially about itself. If you are inclined to say, "No one is as sinful and depraved as I am," be careful that you don't think yourself better than others on this very account. Be careful lest you develop a high opinion of your humility. In essence, if you find yourself thinking often of your humility, it is likely that you have little of it.

In sum, "All gracious affections, that are a sweet odor to Christ, and that fill the soul of a Christian with an heavenly sweetness and fragrancy, are *brokenhearted affections*. A truly Christian love, either to God or men, is a humble brokenhearted love. The desires of the saints, however earnest, are humble desires. Their hope is an humble hope, and their joy, even when it is unspeakable, and full of glory, is a humble, brokenhearted joy, and leaves the Christian more poor in spirit, and more like a little child, and more disposed to an universal lowliness of behavior."

14

THE SEVENTH SIGN OF
AUTHENTIC AFFECTIONS

*Another way in which gracious affections are distinguished
from those that are false is that they are attended with a
change of nature.*

EARLIER WE NOTED THAT all truly gracious and spiritual affections are the result of the revelation to the soul of the excellency and glory of God and divine things. But we must also remember that all such revelations are transforming in their effect. They not only change the sensation and frame of the soul, they also bring to pass an actual alteration in the very nature of the soul.

This is what Paul had in mind when he said in 2 Corinthians 3:18 that "we all, with unveiled face, beholding the glory of the Lord, are being transformed into the same image from one degree of glory to another. For this comes from the Lord who is the Spirit." Any number of things may have an effect on how we think and feel, but God alone changes the nature of the soul itself.

One need only consider the imagery and variety of ways in which the New Testament describes conversion to see that *conversion consists of a profound and deep-seated change of nature.* To be converted is to be born again, to become a new creation; it entails a rising from the dead and being renewed in spirit and mind, a dying to sin and a living to righteousness. To be converted is to put off the old man and to put on the new. To be the subject of God's saving grace is to be ingrafted into a new stock and to have a divine seed implanted in one's heart and to be made a partaker of the divine nature.

It follows, therefore, that "if there be no great and remarkable, abiding change in persons that think they have experienced a work of conversion, vain are all their imaginations and pretenses, however they have been affected." Before being converted, a person may refrain from committing a particular sin. But once he is born of God he not only refrains from committing it but his very heart and nature become averse to it. Merely to abstain from a sin doesn't necessarily mean you are its enemy. But true conversion turns a person away from sin as the soul's mortal enemy.

So, if a person claims to have experienced high and holy affections but, after a season of time, "there is no very sensible, or remarkable alteration in him, as to those bad qualities and evil habits, which before were visible in him, and he is ordinarily under the prevalence of the same kind of dispositions that he used to be, and the same things seem to belong to his character, he appears as selfish, carnal, as stupid, and perverse, as unchristian, and unsavory as ever," it is clear that he is not the object of God's saving grace.

If the change in a person is only temporary and not abiding, it is doubtful whether he has been truly converted. We certainly have to make allowances for a person's natural disposition and temper. In other words, being born again does not entirely root out or eradicate the evil thoughts and sinful habits developed over a lifetime. Thus, those sins that particularly kept a man in bondage before his conversion may well pose an extraordinary threat and danger after his conversion. Still, though, "conversion will make a great alteration even with respect to these sins."

For example, if before his conversion a man was particularly given to sexual immorality or drunkenness or malice, "converting grace will make a great alteration in him, with respect to these evil dispositions, so that however he may be still most in danger of these sins, yet they shall no longer have dominion over him; nor will they any more be properly his character." He may still struggle with such sins and be assaulted by the temptation to indulge them, but the transformation in nature wrought by conversion will have broken the enslaving grip they once exerted on his soul.

Some have argued that they can experience spiritual affections for a time, but that when the affections depart they are left to that condition in which they found themselves before the affections came. In other words, they actually think such affections must be authentic because, when they are absent, they see and feel nothing and are no better off than they were before the affections touched them.

But this is to misunderstand the way God communicates himself and his grace to the human soul. When the Spirit of God comes in conversion, he unites himself to the faculties of the soul and permanently dwells there. The soul cannot help but experience a transformation of nature and not just be the subject of passing experiences or feelings. When the soul of a true believer receives God's light, "its nature is changed, and it becomes properly a luminous thing. Not only does the sun shine in the saints, but they also become little suns, partaking of the nature of the fountain of their light."

The communication of God to the soul releases a divine energy and power that reaches to the depths of the heart and affects its very nature, imparting an abiding divine presence that sustains over a lifetime the gradual renovation of the thoughts and impulses and actions of the soul.

There are certainly high affections of a sort that leave a person unchanged and unaffected once they diminish. But this is by no means the case with those affections that are from God, for "they leave a sweet savor and relish of divine things on the heart, and a stronger bent of soul towards God and holiness." Indeed, when people "have been conversing with Christ in an extraordinary manner, there is a sensible effect of it [that] remains upon them; there is something remarkable in their disposition and frame, which if we take knowledge of, and trace to its cause, we shall find it is because they have been with Jesus."

15

THE EIGHTH SIGN OF AUTHENTIC AFFECTIONS

True religious affections reflect the character of Christ himself. They produce and promote the same love, humility, forgiveness and mercy that we see in Jesus Christ.

ALL THOSE WHO ARE truly godly and regenerate disciples of Jesus Christ have the spirit of Christ in them. Indeed, this spirit not only abides within them but governs and directs and gives shape to their true and proper character.

There are also some virtues that are uniquely Christian and especially give evidence of God's gracious activity. This is because they are especially agreeable to the attributes of God and were extraordinarily manifest in the redemptive work of Christ himself. These virtues are humility, meekness, love, forgiveness, and mercy (see Matt. 11:29). The bottom line is that "Christians are Christlike: none deserve the name of Christians that are not so, in their prevailing character."

This is Paul's point when he says that the new man is renewed after the image of the one who creates him (see Col. 3:10). The elect are predestined to be conformed to the image of the Son of God (see Rom. 8:29). Thus "there is grace in Christians answering to grace in Christ, such an answerableness as there is between the wax and the seal. There is character for character. Such kind of graces, such a spirit and temper, the same things that belong to Christ's character, belong to theirs."

Indeed, it would be strange "if Christians should not be of the same temper and spirit that Christ is of, when they are his flesh and his bone, yea are one spirit (1 Cor. 6:17), and live so, that it is not they that live, but Christ that lives in them. A Christian spirit is Christ's mark that he sets upon the souls of his people; his seal in their foreheads, bearing his image and superscription."

Consider how the Spirit's descent upon Christ as a dove instructs us in this matter. "The dove is a noted emblem of meekness, harmlessness, peace and love. But the same Spirit that descended on the Head of the Church, descends to the members." God has sent forth the same Spirit into our hearts (see Gal. 4:6) such that if any person doesn't have the Spirit he does not belong to Christ (see Rom. 8:9). Christ himself breathes the Spirit into his followers (see John 20:22), the same Spirit with whom all believers have been anointed (see 1 John 2:20, 27).

Let's consider meekness, forgiveness, love, and mercy or compassion in particular. That all Christ's disciples will display a meekness like his is evident from the way he compares them to the temperament of little children (see Matt. 10:42; 18:6, 10, 14; 19:14; John 13:33). Meekness that is a sign of genuine affections entails innocence, harmlessness, the absence of unrighteous anger, guilelessness, simplicity, and a yieldable and flexible spirit.

This is not to deny that there is a place in the Christian heart for fortitude and boldness for Christ. But many misunderstand the nature of this boldness. Like the boldness that was present in Christ himself, it is "an exceeding diverse thing from a brutal fierceness, or the boldness of beasts of prey. True Christian fortitude consists in strength of mind, through grace, exerted in two things: in ruling and suppressing the evil and unruly passions and affections of the mind; and in steadfastly and freely exerting, and following good affections and dispositions, without being hindered by sinful fear, or the opposition of enemies."

Thus the strength and fortitude of the true disciple of Christ "appears in nothing more than in steadfastly maintaining the holy calm, meekness, sweetness, and benevolence of his mind, amidst all the storms, injuries, strange behavior, and surprising acts and events of this evil and unreasonable world."

There is actually a form of boldness that is little more than a disguised version of pride. It's possible for a man to expose himself to the hatred of the world and to provoke its displeasure out of pride rather than out of love for Christ. For it is "the nature of spiritual pride to cause men to seek distinction and singularity; and so oftentimes to set themselves at war with those that they call carnal, that they may be more highly exalted among their party."

The same may be said for that zeal which animates boldness. Yes, Christians are to be a zealous people, on fire for the glory of God, but the flame is "a sweet one, or rather it is the heat and fervor of a sweet flame. For the flame of which it is the heat, is no other than that of divine love, or Christian charity, which is the sweetest and most benevolent thing that is, or can be, in the heart of man or angel."

A true disciple of Christ also has a forgiving spirit and a disposition to overlook and dismiss injuries. Whether we are quick to freely forgive others is actually a sign of whether we have received forgiveness for our own transgressions (see Matt. 6:12–15). This is no less the case with love, for "there is no one virtue or disposition of the mind that is so often and so expressly insisted on, in the marks that are laid down in the New Testament, whereby to know true Christians" (see John 13:34–35; 15:12, 17; 1 John 2:9–10; 3:14).

The Word of God is also unmistakably clear that "none are true saints, but those whose true character it is that they are of a disposition to pity and relieve their fellow creatures that are poor, indigent and afflicted" (see Ps. 37:21, 26; 112:5, 9; Prov. 14:31; 21:26; Jer. 22:16; James 1:27).

There is simply no escaping the fact that Scripture repeatedly declares that "those who are truly gracious are under the government of that lamblike, dovelike spirit of Jesus Christ. . . . We may therefore undoubtedly determine that all truly Christian affections are attended with such a spirit and that this is the natural tendency of the fear and hope, the sorrow and joy, the confidence and the zeal of true Christians."

None of this is meant to suggest that Christians are perfect and sinless, as if regeneration made it impossible for a believer ever to be guilty of being unlike Christ. "But this I affirm, and shall affirm till I deny the Bible to be anything worth, that everything in Christians that belongs to true Christianity is of this tendency, and works this way; and that there is no true Christian upon earth, but is so under the prevailing power of such a spirit, that he is properly denominated from it, and it is truly and justly his character; and that therefore ministers and others have no warrant from Christ to encourage persons that are of a contrary character and behavior, to think they are converted, because they tell a fair story of illumination and discoveries."

Some people are so inclined to identify true religion with "certain transient illuminations and impressions (especially if they are in such a particular method and order) and so little in the spirit and temper persons are of" that they distort Christianity and present a version of it contrary to that in Scripture. "The Scripture knows of no such true Christians, as of a sordid, selfish, cross and contentious spirit."

Certainly we must make allowances for the lingering effects of sin and the habits of a lifetime, but not so "as to allow men, that once were wolves and serpents, to be now converted, without any remarkable change in the spirit of their mind."

So what should we do when a person claims to have experienced a saving encounter with the Spirit and even professes faith in Christ, but fails to display those features of godliness that we've noted in this chapter? Whereas we may not have warrant to tell them they are certainly unregenerate (unless, of course, by some explicit heresy they manifest a heart of unbelief), we should be diligent not to give them what may prove to be a false assurance by saying they are saved.

16

THE NINTH SIGN OF AUTHENTIC AFFECTIONS

True and authentic affections soften the heart and produce a tenderness of spirit and sensitivity toward sin.

FALSE AFFECTIONS, no matter how powerful and moving they may appear to be, have a tendency to harden the human heart toward sin. Those who experience them are so far from being like Jesus Christ that they display an increasing indifference toward their own corruption and selfish self-indulgence.

False affections, over the long haul, tend to stupefy the mind and harden the heart to an awareness of one's past and present sins. They also lead people to be careless in heeding the warnings of Scripture concerning future dangers and transgressions. Such folk are less inclined to discern what is sinful and less afraid of the appearance of evil. Their opinion of themselves is inflated and they lose sight of the urgency of guarding their souls from the temptations of the enemy. They neglect biblical responsibilities they regard as inconvenient and only partially comply with explicit scriptural commands. They are minimally concerned with their own spiritual shortcomings and more easily yield to temptations. They regard themselves as out of danger of hell and thus pay little heed to their behavior or to the more rigorous demands of God's Word.

These people don't view Christ as the Savior *from* sin but as the Savior *of* their sins. Instead of "flying to him as their refuge from their spiritual enemies, they make use of him as the defense of their spiritual enemies, from God, and to strengthen them [i.e., their spiritual enemies] against him." Remarkably, they maintain this posture all the while they "make a great profession of love to God, and assurance of his favor, and great joy in tasting the sweetness of his love." These are the people who turn the grace of God into licentiousness (see Jude 4). They exploit the promise of divine grace to justify their iniquity.

But true, gracious, authentic affections always work to soften and tenderize the heart, making it more aware of sin and the need for divine mercy. Those who are the recipients of God's saving grace are ever filled with a dread of sin and anything that might displease or offend God. They are ever watchful and diligent over their souls lest they be caught up in the deceitfulness of sin.

Jesus compares this tenderness of heart in the true believer to that of a little child. A child's heart is easily moved by concern for spiritual things, is sympathetic toward those in distress, and is always inclined to weep with those who weep. "A little child is easily affected with grief at temporal evils, and has his heart melted, and falls a weeping. Thus, tender is the heart of a Christian with regard to the evil of sin. A little child is easily affrighted at the appearance of outward evils, or anything that threatens its hurt. So is a Christian apt to be alarmed at the appearance of moral evil, and anything that threatens the hurt of the soul. A little child, when it meets enemies, or fierce beasts, is not apt to trust its own strength, but flies to its parents for refuge. So a saint is not self-confident in engaging spiritual enemies, but flies to Christ. A little child is apt to be suspicious of evil in places of danger, afraid in the dark, afraid when left alone, or far from home. So is a saint apt to be sensible of his spiritual dangers, jealous of himself, full of fear when he can't see his way plain before him, afraid to be left alone, and to be at a distance from God. . . . A little child is apt to be afraid of superiors, and to dread their anger, and tremble at their frowns and threatenings. So is a true saint with respect to God. . . . A little child approaches superiors with awe. So do the saints approach God with holy awe and reverence."

As we noted in our discussion of the eighth sign of authentic affections, this childlike spirit is not at all inconsistent with a "holy boldness in prayer and the duties of divine worship." One can be passionate and zealous without sacrificing reverence. Indeed, "no boldness in poor sinful worms of the dust, that have a right sight of God and themselves, will prompt 'em to approach to God with less fear and reverence, than spotless and glorious angels in heaven; who cover their faces before his throne."

One reason why gracious affections are characterized by this tenderness of spirit "is that true grace tends to promote convictions of conscience." The grace of conversion doesn't "stupefy a man's conscience; but makes it more sensible, more easily and thoroughly discerning the sinfulness of that which is sinful, and receiving a greater conviction of the heinous and dreadful nature of sin, susceptive of a quicker and deeper sense of it, and more convinced of his own sinfulness, and wickedness of his heart; and consequently it has a tendency to make him more jealous of his heart. Grace tends to give the soul a further and better conviction of the same things concerning sin, that it was convinced of under a legal work of the Spirit of God."

The heart of the true believer is like a young child who has been burned by fire and now lives in constant fear of it. A counterfeit believer, on the other hand, is like iron that has been quickly heated and then plunged in water, rendering it harder than it ever was before.

Servile fear is banished from the heart of a true believer, as reverential fear of God is increased. The true believer no longer fears future punishment, but ever more fears the mere thought of displeasing the God who has saved him. Fear of hell is gone, while fear of sin is increased. He has an increased distrust of his own native strength, wisdom, and faithfulness. Although his fear of natural evils has diminished, his fear of moral evil has expanded.

Self-confidence is gone, as holy boldness takes its place. "As he is more sure than others of deliverance from hell, so he has more of a sense of the desert of it. He is less apt than others to be shaken in faith; but more apt than others to be moved with solemn warnings, and with God's frowns, and with the calamities of others. He has the firmest comfort, but the softest heart; richer than others, but poorest of all in spirit; the tallest and strongest saint, but the least and most tender child amongst them."

17

THE TENTH SIGN OF
AUTHENTIC AFFECTIONS

Another way in which godly and gracious affections differ from those that are false is in their beautiful symmetry and proportion.

TO DESCRIBE AUTHENTIC affections as beautiful in symmetry and proportion isn't to say that the virtues and inclinations of true saints in this life are perfect or incapable of being improved upon or refined. Indeed, in any number of ways there is the abiding effect of sin on the soul. Although saved, the true believer still lacks instruction, commits errors in judgment, and struggles with the lingering influence of long-standing habits of life. As bad as this may be, however, it is nothing in comparison with the monstrous disproportion that exists in the affections of those who know nothing of saving grace.

One reason for the symmetry and proportion of affections in true saints is that "they have the whole image of Christ upon them." In other words, "there is no grace in Christ, but there is its image in believers to answer it. The image is a true image, and there is something of the same beautiful proportion in the image, which is in the original; there is feature for feature, and member for member. There is symmetry and beauty in God's workmanship."

As for false professors, they often experience great affections in some things but little if any in others. For example, they may display great hope but little reverence or fear. With true believers, on the other hand, "joy and holy fear go together."

True believers experience joy and comfort attended with godly sorrow and mourning for sin. "Although Christ hath borne our griefs, and carried our sorrows, so that we are freed from the sorrow of punishment, and may now sweetly feed upon the comforts Christ hath purchased for us, yet that hinders not but that our feeding on these comforts should be attended with the sorrow of repentance."

Hypocrites, on the other hand, display "a strange partiality and disproportion in the same affections." For example, they may display a passionate love for God but little or no compassion for men. Others will show a great love for their fellow man but virtually no concern for God. Even when there is great love to men, it is disproportionate in that they love some but are bitter toward others. Or if they love their neighbors and pretend to be passionate about Christians who live far off, they fail to love their own wives and are oppressive toward those in their own households.

This disproportion is seen even in the love that false professors have for the same person. "Some men show a love to others as to their outward man, they are liberal of their worldly substance, and often give to the poor, but have no love to, or concern for the souls of men. Others pretend a great love to men's souls [but] are not compassionate and charitable towards their bodies. . . . But a true Christian love to our brethren, extends both to their souls and bodies. And herein is like the love and compassion of Jesus Christ." He loved men's souls and their bodies.

Another example is when a person is greatly disturbed by the spiritual defects of other Christians but is oblivious to his own. "A true Christian," on the other hand, "may be affected with the coldness and unsavoriness of other saints, and may mourn much over it. But at the same time he is not so apt to be affected with the badness of anybody's heart, as his own."

Often those who are the subject of false affections will profess to having attained great spiritual heights but will have failed to walk faithfully in lesser duties. They insist they live on a higher spiritual plane than most, yet fail to manifest the basic virtues of a biblically moral life. Or they profess to be greatly touched with their own wickedness but feel nothing when they violate the basic commands in God's Word.

They say they are willing to be damned for God's glory but refuse to sacrifice anything of their physical comforts on earth for the sake of fulfilling their biblical duties. They make noise about having trusted their souls to Christ and looking to him alone for their eternal welfare, but don't have enough confidence in God to trust him with their earthly welfare by giving generously to those in need.

True believers hate all sin and are zealous in their resistance to sin in general. The false, on the other hand, display a zeal only against some particular sins. They may zealously resist profanity or ostentatious dress, but are given over to covetousness and backbiting and ill will toward those who have injured them.

"False zeal is against the sins of others, while men have no zeal against their own sins. But he that has true zeal exercises it chiefly against his own sins."

False believers display an inconsistency and inconstancy in their battle with sin. Their spiritual experience is by fits and starts; at one moment they are up and seem raised above clouds in their affections, "and then suddenly fall down again, lose all, and become quite careless and carnal, and this is their manner of carrying on religion." They tend to be greatly moved spiritually only in times of revival or during seasons of remarkable divine providence or on those occasions when they claim to be the recipient of a significant divine revelation. But they quickly revert to former ways at ordinary times and "the prevailing bent of their hearts and stream of their affections is ordinarily toward the things of this world." They are like the Israelites, who were spiritually excited upon being set free from Egypt and delivered through the waters of the Red Sea, only to lust after what they left behind and immediately turn to worshiping a golden calf.

They are like "the waters in the time of a shower of rain, which during the shower, and a little after, run like a brook, and flow abundantly, but are presently quite dry; and when another shower comes, then they will flow again. Whereas a true saint is like a stream from a living spring, which though it may be greatly increased by a shower of rain, and diminished in time of drought, yet constantly runs."

Hypocrites are like comets "that appear for a while with a mighty blaze, but are very unsteady and irregular in their motion . . . and their blaze soon disappears, and they appear but once in a great while. But the true saints are like the fixed stars, which, though they rise and set, and are often clouded, yet are steadfast in their orb, and may truly be said to shine with a constant light."

Those who are subject to false affections also display an unevenness and disproportion in the timing of their experience. They typically are affected when in the company of others but not when they are in secret, in silent meditation and prayer, when alone and separated from the world. "A true Christian doubtless delights in religious fellowship, and Christian conversation, and finds much to affect his heart in it. But he also delights at times to retire from all mankind, to converse with God in solitary places."

When a person is in the grip of true, godly affections he often longs to be alone, to find seasons and places of solitude so that he might meditate on God and his Word and pour out his heart in prayer and praise. This was especially true of Jesus. "How often do we read of his retiring into mountains and solitary places for holy converse with his Father?" The fact is, gracious affections are by nature more silent and secret than those that are counterfeit. The latter tend to be boisterous and seek to be noticed by others.

Scripture consistently indicates that "the most eminent divine favors that the saints obtained . . . were in their retirement," which is to say, when they withdrew from others and sought God in the secret place. Such was the case with Abraham, Isaac, Jacob, Moses, Elijah and Elisha, as well as Jesus.

"But this is all that I aim at by what has been said, to show that it is the nature of true grace, that however it loves Christian society in its place, yet it in a particular manner delights in retirement, and secret converse with God. So that if persons appear greatly engaged in social religion, and but little in the religion of the closet, and are often highly affected when with others, and but little moved when they have none but God and Christ to converse with, it looks very darkly upon their religion."

18

THE ELEVENTH SIGN OF AUTHENTIC AFFECTIONS

When genuine, gracious affections are experienced in high degree, it serves only to intensify one's longing for more. False affections, on the other hand, rest satisfied in themselves.

THERE IS A POWERFUL dynamic at work in the experience of genuine, gracious affections in which the more one tastes the activity of the Spirit, the hungrier one becomes. The more one drinks from the well of Christ's beauty, the thirstier he is. "The more a true saint loves God with a gracious love, the more he desires to love him, and the more uneasy is he at his want [i.e., lack] of love to him. The more he hates sin, the more he desires to hate it, and laments that he has so much remaining love to it. The more he mourns for sin, the more he longs to mourn for sin. The more his heart is broken, the more he desires it should be broken. The more he thirsts and longs after God and holiness, the more he longs to long, and breathe out his very soul in longings after God. The kindling and raising of gracious affections is like kindling a flame: the higher it is raised, the more ardent it is; and the more it burns, the more vehemently does it tend and seek to burn."

Here is the principle in view: "The greatest eminency and perfection that the saints arrive to in this world, has no tendency to satiety, or to abate their desires after more; but on the contrary, makes them more eager to press forwards." The reason for this is that the more one experiences genuine affections, the more one develops a spiritual taste by which one perceives the excellency and relishes the divine sweetness of holiness. Furthermore, the more grace one has, the more one senses the imperfection and emptiness in one's self and thus the distance from what he ought to have; and thus he sees his great need of grace. Such folk are thus more inclined to pursue spiritual growth and to avail themselves of whatever means are proper and helpful to attain it.

Someone may object and say that this is inconsistent with the biblical declaration that spiritual enjoyments are satisfying to the soul. If they are, how can it be that the more one tastes of them, the more one senses how little he has and how much more he needs? To answer this we must explain in what sense spiritual enjoyments are said to be of a soul-satisfying nature.

(1) In the first place, these delights are so perfectly adapted to the nature, capacity, and need of the human soul that "those who find them, desire no other kind of enjoyments." Once you've tasted the spiritual sweetness of Christ and the soul-satisfying pleasure he imparts, you are ruined for anything else. The soul is no longer tempted to wander, looking for competing pleasures, nor inclined to change.

(2) They are also satisfying in that "they answer the expectation of the appetite." This expectation cannot be satisfied by "worldly enjoyments." Spiritual enjoyments "fully answer and satisfy the expectation."

(3) The gratification and pleasure spiritual enjoyments bring is permanent, but this is not so with worldly or carnal pleasures. The latter "in a sense satisfy particular appetites; but the appetite in being satisfied, is glutted, and then the pleasure is over, and as soon as that is over, the general appetite of human nature after happiness returns, but is empty, and without anything to satisfy it. So that the glutting of a particular appetite does but take away from, and leave empty, the general thirst of nature."

(4) Finally, spiritual enjoyments are capable of satisfying the soul, if obstacles to them are removed, to such a degree that nothing else is required. There is an ocean of satisfaction in spiritual delights if the soul would but extend itself to drink it in. Thus "the more he [i.e., the believer] experiences, and the more he knows this excellent, unparalleled, exquisite, and satisfying sweetness, the more earnestly will he hunger and thirst for more, till he comes to perfection."

But it is not so with false affections. The great desire that once existed, after the experience of false affections, ceases or is abated. A person might have once longed for spiritual light and to love God. Then, having experienced false affections, he is deceived and led to believe that this is enough and that his spiritual state is sure and safe. Thus his longings for more disappear under the deception that he has all he needs and will go to heaven regardless of what occurs. "And especially when false affections are raised very high, do they put an end to longings after grace and holiness. The man now is far from appearing to himself a poor empty creature. On the contrary, he is rich, and increased with goods, and hardly conceives of anything more excellent than what he has already attained to."

This is why Scripture often portrays seeking God as a sign of the true saint (see Ps. 24:6; 69:6, 32; 70:4). In fact, the Bible more often than not portrays this seeking as the characteristic of a saint *after* his conversion more than before.

There will always be some false professors who will insist that they long for more and do not want to rest content with past achievements. "But the truth is, their desires are not properly the desires of appetite after holiness, for its own sake, or for the moral excellency and holy sweetness that is in it, but only for by-ends [i.e., by-products, or the good effects they think they can achieve by means of such desire]."

For example, they may long for revelations from God only so that they may be satisfied with the state of their soul. Or they long for illumination concerning God's love because they desire to be made much of by God rather than to make much of God. Or they fancy themselves longing for more grace lest they be looked upon badly by others for resting satisfied with what they have. But in the true saint there is a natural and instinctive longing after God and holiness for their own sake. "And holiness or sanctification is more directly the object of it [i.e., of the desire and panting and longing for more] than any manifestation of God's love and favor."

The true children of God "desire the sincere milk of the Word, not so much to testify God's love to them, as that they may grow thereby in holiness." Hypocrites, on the other hand, "long for discoveries, more for the present comfort of the discovery, and the high manifestation of God's love in it, than for any sanctifying influence of it."

19

THE TWELFTH SIGN OF AUTHENTIC AFFECTIONS (1)

Gracious and holy affections always bear the fruit of holiness of life.

THIS IS NOT ONLY THE most important of the twelve signs of the saving presence of the Spirit but the most controversial as well. In order for us to grasp what is in view, we need to make three observations.

First, it is necessary that a person be "universally obedient." This does not mean the regenerate are perfect or sinless. What it does mean is that they are willing and devoted to parting ways with all "their dearest iniquities." There is no element or facet of our responsibility to Christ that we feel ourselves exempt from pursuing. This extends not only to the avoidance of all sins that are noted in Scripture but also to the positive practice of those virtues we read of in God's Word.

Second, if a person is a true Christian he or she will pursue the business of religion and the service of God "with great earnestness and diligence, as the work which they devote themselves to, and make the main business of their lives." Those whom Christ redeemed are said to be zealous for good works (see Titus 2:14), which is to say their hearts are fully employed and engaged in the practice of righteousness. "The kingdom of heaven is not to be taken but by violence. Without earnestness there is no getting along in that narrow way that leads to life, and so no arriving at that state of glorious life and happiness which it leads to."

Without "earnest labor" and "constant laboriousness" there is no hope of finally and fully attaining to eternal life. "Slothfulness in the service of God, in his professed servants, is as damning as open rebellion."

Third, every true Christian "perseveres in this way of universal obedience, and diligent and earnest service of God, through all the various kinds of trials that he meets with, to the end of life." Such perseverance is not the sort that is easily attained when times are smooth and successful. This is a perseverance that occurs through trials and temptations and the worst of times.

Many things serve to derail us from godly perseverance in the pursuit of righteousness: the alluring appeal of sin, those things that remove the restraints on the expression of our sinful inclinations, and especially those things that make the performance of duty appear hard, unappealing, and terrible, such as the suffering, reproach, contempt, pain, and loss of possessions and outward comforts we incur if we stay in the way of righteousness. Indeed, often God in his providence so orders our lives that these trials come our way to bring to the surface the true nature of our commitment and the depth of our conviction.

None of what has just been said should be taken to mean that true saints cannot backslide or fall into sin. But "they can never fall away so as to grow weary of religion and the service of God, and habitually to dislike it and neglect it, either on its own account, or on account of the difficulties that attend it."

True saints can never backslide so far that they abandon the way of righteousness altogether. "Nor can they ever fall away so as habitually to be more engaged in other things than in the business of religion, or so that it should become their way and manner to serve something else more than God."

Nor can a true saint ever fall away to the extent "that it shall come to this, that ordinarily there shall be no remarkable difference in his walk and behavior since his conversion, from what was before. They that are truly converted are new men, new creatures; new, not only within, but without; they are sanctified throughout, in spirit, soul and body. Old things are passed away, all things are become new. They have new hearts, and new eyes, new ears, new tongues, new hands, new feet, i.e. a new conversation and practice, and they walk in newness of life and continue to do so to the end of life. And they that fall away, and cease visibly to do so, 'tis a sign they never were risen with Christ. And especially when men's opinion of their being converted, and so in a safe estate, is the very cause of their coming to this, it is a most evident sign of their hypocrisy."

Why is it that gracious affections will always result in godly practice? Because God has communicated himself to us in our experience of being born again. We participate in the divine nature. Christ lives in our hearts. The Holy Spirit dwells within and unites himself to our faculties as an internal vital principle and exerts his nature in the exercise of our faculties of soul. How could divine omnipotence, dwelling in the human soul, fail to be powerful and effectual in the production of a godly life?

In other words, if God dwells in the heart and is vitally united to it, "he will show that he is a God, by the efficacy of his operation. Christ is not in the heart of a saint as in a sepulcher, or as a dead Savior, that does nothing, but as in his temple, and as one that is alive from the dead. For in the heart where Christ savingly is, there he lives, and exerts himself after the power of that endless life that he received at his resurrection."

The spirit of Christ, "which is the immediate spring of grace in the heart, is all life, all power, all act" (see especially 1 Cor. 2:4; 1 Thess. 1:5; 1 Cor. 4:20). This is why saving affections, although not as loud or visible as others, have in them "a secret solidity, life and strength, whereby they take hold of and carry away the heart, leading it into a kind of captivity (2 Cor. 10:5), gaining a full and steadfast determination of the will for God and holiness." Thus, holy affections "have a governing power in the course of a man's life."

A granite statue may have all the external features of a real person, representing well the contours of his body and appearance. But there is no inward principle or power to animate and supply strength. Thus it does nothing, and accomplishes nothing. "But gracious affections go to the very bottom of the heart and take hold of the very inmost springs of life and activity." True and gracious affections conquer the will and triumph over lusts and corruptions of nature and carry us into the way of holiness despite all temptations, difficulty, and opposition.

There are numerous reasons why truly gracious affections issue in godly practice, virtually all of which are related to the eleven signs of authentic spirituality we have already examined. Let's take note of just a few of them.

For example, one reason why people with holy affections are given to holy practice is because what they seek is God himself, solely for the excellency of who he is, and not whatever good uses or ends the knowledge of God might bring them. If a person seeks God only for the benefits he brings us, once those benefits disappear or fail to materialize, one's hunger for God likewise diminishes. This is why gracious affections will enable men to persevere in the pursuit of godliness even when it is painful to do so. If the pursuit of godliness comes at great cost to a person's comfort and private interests, the unregenerate will abandon the former for the sake of the latter. But he who loves God for God's own sake will be so impelled by the beauty and excellency of his divine nature that no degree of trial or loss will impede him.

Again, once we grasp the moral excellence of divine things or the beauty of holiness, we can better understand why one is committed to persevere in the practice of godliness. "Seeing [that] holiness is the main thing that excites, draws and governs all gracious affections, no wonder that all such affections tend to holiness. That which men love, they desire to have and to be united to, and possessed of. That beauty which men delight in, they desire to be adorned with. Those acts which men delight in, they necessarily incline to do."

We must also remember that the Spirit of God in teaching and leading the believer "gives the soul a natural relish of the sweetness of that which is holy, and of everything that is holy, so far as it comes in view, and excites a disrelish and disgust of everything that is unholy." If a person should find himself relishing and delighting in that which is unholy, along with distasting and disregarding that which is spiritually excellent, there is reason to doubt that he ever has been the subject of a gracious and saving activity of the Holy Spirit.

The nature of that spiritual knowledge which comes with conversion also accounts for why those with authentic affections will persevere in godly practice. "By the sight of the transcendent glory of Christ, true Christians see him worthy to be followed, and so are powerfully drawn after him. They see him worthy that they should forsake all for him. By the sight of that superlative amiableness, they are thoroughly disposed to be subject to him, and engaged to labor with earnestness and activity in his service, and made willing to go through all difficulties for his sake. And 'tis the discovery of this divine excellency of Christ that makes them constant to him, for it makes a deep impression upon their minds that they cannot forget him, and they will follow him whithersoever he goes, and it is in vain for any to endeavor to draw them away from him."

Also, the thorough conviction or certainty of a soul in the truth of divine things impels true believers to godly practice. If some are never thoroughly convinced of the truth of the gospel, it is no wonder they fall to the side when trials and afflictions arise. But it is different with those who are fully assured of the gospel truth, "for the things revealed in the Word of God are so great, and so infinitely more important, than all other things, that it is inconsistent with the human nature, that a man should fully believe the truth of them, and not be influenced by them above all things, in his practice."

We can also point to what we said of humility. A proud spirit is rebellious and resistant to the things of God, whereas a humble spirit yields and is subject to the commands of Scripture. The humble commit themselves to God and subject their will and soul to his ways.

It's inconceivable that divine grace would not bear the fruit of godly practice, for "there is nothing in heaven or earth of a more active nature; for 'tis life itself." There is nothing in the universe that has a greater and more effectual tendency to produce fruit than grace. "Godliness in the heart has as direct a relation to practice as a fountain has to a stream, or as the luminous nature of the sun has to beams sent forth, or as life has to breathing, or the beating of the pulse, or any other vital act; or as a habit or principle of action has to action, for it is the very nature and notion of grace that it is a principle of holy action or practice."

Indeed, it is the very nature and purpose of regeneration and conversion by grace that godly practice should result (see Eph. 2:10; Titus 2:14; 2 Cor. 5:15; Heb. 9:14; Col. 1:21–22; 1 Pet. 1:18; Luke 1:74–75; John 15:13; Eph. 1:4). Thus "holy practice is as much the end of all that God does about his saints, as fruit is the end of all the husbandman does about the growth of his field or vineyard."

The unsaved are often inclined to promise godly practice and even to humble themselves to some extent when they are confronted with the manifestation of God's judgment and discipline, but they never wholly give themselves to holiness. Under pressure of the plagues, Pharaoh gave some indication of his willingness to let the people go, but would later renege on his commitment. He appeared willing to obey God yet held on to his sins. "So it oftentimes is with sinners: they are willing to part with some of their sins, but not all. They are brought to part with the more gross acts of sin, but not to part with their lusts, in lesser indulgences of them."

Even though Pharaoh was under great judgment and a sense of divine wrath when he consented and let the people go, he soon reverted to his natural instincts and pursued them to the Red Sea, intent on destroying them. The reason is that "those lusts of pride and covetousness that were gratified by Pharaoh's dominion over the people, and the gains of their service, were never really mortified in him, but only violently restrained. . . . Thus there may be a forced parting with ways of disobedience to the commands of God, that may seem to be universal, as to what appears for a little season, but because 'tis a mere force, without the mortification of the inward principle of sin, they will not persevere in it, but will return as the dog to its vomit."

We will continue with a summary of this sign of authentic affections in the next chapter.

20

THE TWELFTH SIGN OF
AUTHENTIC AFFECTIONS (2)

Gracious and holy affections always bear the fruit of holiness of life.

AS WE NOTED AT THE beginning of our analysis of this final sign of authentic affections, it is both the most important and controversial of all the signs that we have studied. In fact, we may even go so far to say that godly practice "is the *chief* of all the signs of grace, both as an evidence of the sincerity of professors unto others, and also to their own consciences."

First, we consider how godly practice is a manifestation to others of the truth of one's profession of Christ.

Consider Matthew 7:16, 20; and 12:33. "Christ nowhere says, ye shall know the tree by its leaves or flowers, or ye shall know men by their talk, or ye shall know them by the good story they tell of their experiences, or ye shall know them by the manner and air of their speaking, and emphasis and pathos of expression, or by their speaking feelingly, or by making a very great show by abundance of talk, or by many tears and affectionate expressions, or by the affections ye feel in your hearts towards them. But by their fruits shall ye know them; the tree is known by its fruit; every tree is known by its own fruit."

Not only is this the way we judge of others, it is also the way others are to judge the sincerity of our profession (see Matt. 5:16). "Christ doesn't say that others hearing your good words, your good story, or your pathetical expressions, but 'that others seeing your good works may glorify your Father which is in heaven.'" We also see this in Philippians 2:21–22; 3 John 3–6; and James 2:18.

"Now certainly all accounts we give of ourselves in words, our saying that we have faith, and that we are converted, and telling the manner how we came to have faith, and the steps by which it was wrought, and the discoveries and experiences that accompanied it, are still but manifesting our faith by what we say. 'Tis but showing our faith by our words, which the Apostle speaks of as falling vastly short of manifesting of it by what we do, and showing our faith by our works."

Not only does Scripture clearly teach that works are better than words in showing the state of one's soul, reason also dictates this to be the case.

If a man professes his love and his undying friendship for another, reason teaches that merely saying so is a poor proof of its reality. But if he is constant and faithful and sacrificial in aiding his friend, always ready to lay down his life on his behalf, then his words are given greater weight. The same is true in our relationship with Christ (see John 14:21). If a person throughout life follows and imitates Christ and denies himself for the glory of Christ and promotes the kingdom of Christ, reason indicates this is a sure sign of his truly loving Christ. Testimonies and great stories and fervent declarations are only as good as the practice of godliness and love that follows.

If a man loudly declares that his heart is weaned from the world and that he regards it as vanity and professes to give up all to follow God, but in his practice is fervent in his pursuit of worldly things and holds closely to what he gains and is reluctant to part with it for the sake of charity toward those in need, it is nothing to compare with the one who freely and happily gives away all to bless those in need and is quick to forsake everything for the sake of the kingdom. Thus "reason teaches that the latter gives far the most credible manifestation of an heart weaned from the world."

Passing, spurious affections "easily produce words, and words are cheap; and godliness is more easily feigned in words than in actions. Christian practice is a costly laborious thing. The self-denial that is required of Christians, and the narrowness of the way that leads to life, don't consist in words, but in practice. Hypocrites may much more easily be brought to *talk* like saints than to *act* like saints."

This isn't to suggest that a verbal profession of Christ isn't necessary and important. In all these declarations of the necessity of godly
practice, "a profession of Christianity is plainly presupposed. It is not
the main thing in the evidence, nor anything distinguishing in it, yet 'tis
a thing requisite and necessary in it." So that "if any man should say
plainly that he was not a Christian, and did not believe that Jesus was
the Son of God, or a person sent of God, these rules of Christ and his
apostles don't at all oblige us to look upon him as a sincere Christian,
let his visible practice and virtues be what they will."

But what actually constitutes a Christian profession? First, "there
must undoubtedly be a profession of all that is necessary to his being
a Christian, or of so much as belongs to the essence of Christianity.
Whatsoever is essential in Christianity itself, the profession of that is
essential in the profession of Christianity." This isn't to say that it is
necessary "that there should be an explicit profession of every individual thing that belongs to Christian grace or virtue, but certainly
there must be a profession, either express or implicit, of what is of the
essence of religion."

Things that must be professed, for example, include repentance
of sin, faith in Christ as the only savior from sin, reliance on Christ's
righteousness alone, devotion to him alone, "and that they rejoice in
him as their only righteousness and portion." They ought to profess
their willingness to embrace Christianity with all its attendant difficulties, to walk in the way of obedience without exception, and to serve
and love Christ forever.

Second, the profession must be made with understanding. People
must be sufficiently instructed in the faith so that they know the meaning and intent of all they profess to be true.

Contrary to what some have argued, part of this profession need
not be the particular steps and method by which the Spirit awakened
their hearts to the truth of the faith. Yes, they must be able to give an
account of their experience to others. They must profess to an awareness of their sin and just condemnation before God, that they fully trust
in Christ as the one who has satisfied this divine wrath on their behalf,
that their souls wholly cleave to him alone for rest and refuge, that
they utterly repent of their sins and willingly submit to Christ as king,
and that they renounce the enjoyments of this world and look exclu-

sively to the glories of heaven that God has promised. What we must acknowledge as unscriptural, however, "is the insisting on a particular account of the distinct method and steps wherein the Spirit of God did sensibly proceed, in first bringing the soul into a state of salvation, as a thing requisite in order to receiving a professor into full charity as a real Christian."

Third, notwithstanding the importance of all that has been said in the first two points concerning the necessity of godly practice as evidence of sincerity, there are "no external manifestations and outward appearances whatsoever, that are visible to the world, [which] are infallible evidences of grace." Yes, it is true that such outward behavior, when joined with verbal profession, should lead us to treat as saints those who embody them. "But nothing that appears to them in their neighbor, can be sufficient to beget an absolute certainty concerning the state of his soul, for they see not his heart, nor can they see all his external behavior; for much of it is in secret, and hid from the eye of the world." And it is impossible to know absolutely how far a person might go in performing such deeds from other principles or for other goals than that of love to God.

Having shown that godly practice is the best evidence of the sincerity of one's profession of faith, we now turn, secondly, to observe how Scripture speaks of godly practice as a sure evidence of grace to a person's own conscience.

This is John's point in 1 John 2:3. The testimony of our conscience with respect to good deeds gives us assurance of our own godliness (see also 1 John 3:18–19; Gal. 6:4; Ps. 119:6).

Why is it that one's actions are the best and most effective of all signs of sincerity in religion? Reason itself demonstrates that what a person actually does in any moment of decision is the best indication of what his heart prefers. In other words, "a man's actions are the proper trial [of] what a man's heart prefers." The best test of what is in a man's heart is the actual moment of choice when he is confronted with the world on the one hand and God on the other. Choosing God is the proof of what he professes to be in his heart. "Godliness consists not in an heart to intend to do the will of God, but in an heart to do it."

It is therefore "absurd, and even ridiculous, for any to pretend that they have a good heart while they live a wicked life, or don't bring forth the fruit of universal holiness in their practice. . . . Men that live in ways of sin, and yet flatter themselves that they shall go to heaven, or expect to be received hereafter as holy persons, without a holy life and practice, act as though they expected to make a fool of their Judge."

This is Paul's point in Galatians 6:7. He is, in effect, saying, "Don't deceive yourselves with an expectation of reaping life everlasting hereafter, if you don't sow to the Spirit here; 'tis in vain to think that God will be made a fool of by you, that he will be shamed and baffled with shadows instead of substance, and with vain pretense, instead of that good fruit which he expects, when the contrary to what you pretend appears plainly in your life, before his face."

But our great God and Judge, "whose eyes are as a flame of fire, will not be mocked or baffled with any pretenses, without a holy life. If in his name men have prophesied and wrought miracles, and have had faith, so that they could remove mountains, and cast out devils, and however high their religious affections have been, however great resemblances they have had of grace, and though their hiding place has been so dark and deep that no human skill nor search could find them out, yet if they are workers or practicers of iniquity, they can't hide their hypocrisy from their Judge."

That which truly proves whether men prefer God to the world are those difficulties and trials that make it hard to pursue godliness. When we are faced with a decision in which it is impossible to hold both to God and the world, and holding to God comes at great cost and pain, and yet we do so, such is proof that we truly prefer him in our hearts and that our profession is sincere and saving. Countless times in Scripture we see various trials and difficulties set forth as a way of making evident what is truly in the heart (see Deut. 8:2; Judg. 2:21–22; James 1:2–3; 1 Pet. 1:6–7; 2 Cor. 8:8; Ps. 66:10–11; Zech. 13:9).

"For when God is said by these things to try men, and prove them, to see what is in their hearts, and whether they will keep his commandments or not, we are not to understand that it is for his own information, or that he may obtain evidence himself of their sincerity (for he needs no trials for his information); but chiefly for *their* conviction, and to exhibit evidence to *their* consciences."

We also see instances in Scripture where grace is said to be made perfect or brought to completion or finished by godly practice. Thus the latter is evidence of the former (see James 2:22; 1 John 2:4–5; 4:12). To this we add the numerous references to love and obedience as proof of saving grace: John 14:15, 23–24; 15:2, 8, 14; 8:31; 1 John 2:3, 5; 3:18–19.

Godly practice or holiness of life "is the grand evidence which will hereafter be made use of, before the judgment seat of God, according to which his judgment will be regulated and the state of every professor of religion unalterably determined." One need only consider Revelation 20:12–13; 2 Corinthians 5:10; and countless other texts in which works are the criteria by which the state of men's souls is judged. "Certainly that which our supreme Judge will chiefly make use of to judge us by, when we come to stand before him, we should chiefly make use of to judge ourselves by."

From all that we have seen, we may derive the following summary statements concerning godly practice:

(1) Godly practice and holiness of life and thought is the proper proof of the true and saving knowledge of God. It is both vain and presumptuous for us to profess that we know God if in works we deny him (see Titus 1:16; 1 John 2:3).

(2) Godly and holy practice provides solid evidence that we have truly repented (see Matt. 3:8; Acts 26:20).

(3) Holiness of life is evidence of a saving faith and a confident belief of the truth of all God has revealed (see James 2:21–24; 3 John 3). Or again, it "is the most proper evidence of a true coming to Christ, and accepting of, and closing with him" for salvation.

(4) Godly practice functions as evidence "of a gracious love, both to God and men."

(5) Holiness of life gives evidence of authentic humility (see Mic. 6:8), the true fear or reverence of God, together with a heart filled with gratitude for blessings received (see Ps. 116:12).

(6) Practice is the proper evidence of gracious desires and longings and distinguishes them from those that are false and vain.

(7) "Practice is the proper evidence of a gracious hope."

(8) "A cheerful practice of our duty and doing the will of God, is the proper evidence of a truly holy joy."

(9) Finally, "practice also is the proper evidence of Christian fortitude."

But don't we judge the reality of our profession from our "inward spiritual experiences"? Yes, but such experience is always connected with and produces outward behavior. It is possible for there to be external practice that has no relation to inward convictions. Such mechanical "obedience" is useless. And there is also inward experience that is unaccompanied by outward behavior, which is also of no use. But true inward experience will always manifest itself in outward practice such that the latter is that by which we are to judge the validity and sincerity of the former.

It is undeniable that being sealed with the Spirit of God in our hearts is a great experience that bears witness to the reality of our saving relationship to the Father. But God himself gives witness to and sets his seal upon such an experience when we engage universally and with perseverance in godly practice.

Another objection often heard is that to place so much emphasis on the necessity of godly practice as the evidence of saving grace is to magnify human works. Such emphasis will only serve to diminish the glory of divine grace and threaten the truth of justification by faith alone.

But good works are a threat to divine grace *only* if they are the price we pay to gain it, not if they are the sign of its presence. If a beggar looks at the money just given to him as a sign of the generosity of the one who gave it, he does not regard it as the price he himself paid to gain such favor, nor does it compromise the kindness on the part of the giver.

"The notion of the freeness of the grace of God to sinners, as that is revealed and taught in the gospel, is not that no holy and amiable qualifications or actions in us shall be a fruit, and so a sign of that grace." Rather, the point is "that it is not the worthiness or loveliness of any qualification or action of ours which recommends us to that grace; that kindness is shown to the unworthy and unlovely; that there is great excellency in the benefit bestowed, and no excellency in the subject as the price of it; that goodness goes forth and flows out, from the fullness of God's nature, the fullness of the Fountain of Good, without any amiableness in the object to draw it."

When Scripture says we are justified by grace and not by works, the point is that there is nothing worthy or amiable in what we do that attains for us Christ and his saving benefits. "But that the worthiness or amiableness of nothing in us recommends and brings us to an interest in Christ, is no argument that nothing in us is a sign of an interest in Christ."

I grant that "it would be [legalism] to suppose that holy practice justifies by bringing us to a title to Christ's benefits, as the price of it, or as recommending to it by its preciousness or excellence; but it is not [legalism] to suppose that holy practice justifies the sincerity of a believer, as the proper evidence of it."

PART TWO

Personal Narrative

Introduction

THE PERSONAL SPIRITUALITY
OF JONATHAN EDWARDS

OF ALL THAT Jonathan Edwards wrote, including the *Religious Affections*, nothing provides the penetrating gaze into his own soul, together with his spiritual struggles and triumphs, as does his *Personal Narrative*. This is the closest thing in the vast corpus of Edwardsean writings to what we today would call a "personal testimony."

The *Narrative* was written sometime in 1740 (Edwards was thirty-seven years old at the time) and provides a remarkable view of the reflections of Edwards on the nature of his own relationship with God.[1] Surprisingly, Edwards probably never intended for his *Personal Narrative* to be published, or for you and me, or anyone else for that matter (beyond his closest friends), to read it.[2]

---

[1]All agree that the *Personal Narrative* was written before *Religious Affections*. Daniel B. Shea suggested that "it might conceivably have been written as Edwards prepared a series of sermons given in 1742–1743, on which the *Religious Affections* is based. The only absolute certainty," noted Shea, "is that he did not conclude the narrative before January 1739, the date he mentions in its final paragraph" (Daniel B. Shea, "The Art and Instruction of Jonathan Edwards' *Personal Narrative*," in *Critical Essays on Jonathan Edwards,* ed. William J. Scheick [Boston: G. K. Hall & Co., 1980], 275; originally published in *American Literature* 37 [March 1965]: 17–32). We have since come to know with a fair degree of certainty that the *Narrative* was written in response to a request from Edwards' future son-in-law Aaron Burr. George Claghorn cites a letter to Edwards in 1741 in which Burr thanks him for his letter of December 14, 1740. Burr then adds: "I desire to bless God that he inclined you to write and especially to write so freely of your own experiences; I think it has been much blessed to my spiritual good. Though I have often heard and read of others' experiences, I never [met] with'm anything that had the like effect upon me. It came in a most seasonable time, and was the means of clearing up several things that I was in the dark about'" (cited in George S. Claghorn, introduction to "Personal Writings," in Jonathan Edwards, *Letters and Personal Writings,* ed. George S. Claghorn, vol. 16 of The Works of Jonathan Edwards [New Haven, Conn.: Yale University Press, 1998], 747).

[2]The *Narrative* was first published by Samuel Hopkins in 1765, seven years after Edwards' death. It is less than seven thousand words in length and, according to Shea, "gives the appearance of hurried writing. But if Edwards spent only a day with his spiritual autobiography, he had spent twenty years or more arriving at the criteria by which he judged his experience" (Shea, "Art and Instruction," 266). The text of the *Narrative* can be found in numerous editions of Edwards' works. I use the version made available at www.JonathanEdwards.com. One can also find the *Narrative* in Edwards, *Letters and Personal Writings* (ed. Claghorn); and in *A Jonathan Edwards Reader,* ed. John E. Smith, Harry S. Stout, and Kenneth P. Minkema (New Haven, Conn.: Yale University Press, 1995), 281–296. Another edition is contained in *The Works of Jonathan Edwards,* ed. Edward

What, then, if any, is the relationship between the *Affections* and the *Personal Narrative?* Only this, but assuredly this: that the principles found in the former we now see in Edwards' own experience. Much of the language and imagery, and certainly the theology, of the *Personal Narrative* later reappear in *Religious Affections,* as one might expect. Therefore, my purpose in providing the text of the *Narrative,* together with my brief observations, is that you might see a personal and vibrant embodiment of the "signs of the Spirit" in Edwards himself.

This is Daniel Shea's point in saying that by narrative example Edwards "will teach what is false and what is true in religious experience, giving another form to the argument he carried on elsewhere [principally in the *Affections*]; and he hopes to affect his readers by both the content and the presentation of his exemplary experience."[3] More recent Edwardsean scholarship concurs. George Claghorn argues that "Edwards edited his own experience to fit his prescription of the model saint,"[4] while Charles Hambrick-Stowe describes the *Narrative* as "a carefully crafted account of Edwards' spiritual pilgrimage, charting, in the words of one of his earlier sermons, his progress on the 'journey towards heaven.'"[5]

I dare say that nothing I have read in the history of Christian spirituality compares with Edwards when it comes to expressions of love for Christ and descriptions of divine beauty and yearnings of the heart for holiness and humility. You won't always agree with Edwards, but even where you differ with him you'll be challenged and instructed.

The Spirituality of the Personal Narrative

As a way of preparing you for what is to come, allow me to cite ten characteristics of the religious life that we see in Edwards himself.[6]

Hickman, 2 vols. (Carlisle, Pa.: Banner of Truth, 1979), 1:xii–xv, xlvi–xlviii. For a brief history of the many reprinted editions of the *Narrative,* see George S. Claghorn, introduction to "Personal Writings," in Edwards, *Letters and Personal Writings* (ed. Claghorn), 751–752; and Shea, "Art and Instruction," 80, n. 1.

[3]Shea, "Art and Instruction," 266.

[4]Claghorn, introduction to "Personal Writings," in Edwards, *Letters and Personal Writings* (ed. Claghorn), 748.

[5]Charles Hambrick-Stowe, "The 'Inward, Sweet Sense' of Christ in Jonathan Edwards," in *The Legacy of Jonathan Edwards: American Religion and the Evangelical Tradition,* ed. D. G. Hart, Sean Michael Lucas, and Stephen J. Nichols (Grand Rapids, Mich.: Baker, 2003), 79.

[6]I have been greatly helped in my understanding of the *Narrative* by the work of Michael J. McClymond in his *Encounters with God: An Approach to the Theology of Jonathan Edwards* (New York: Oxford University Press, 1998), especially 37–49.

First, Edwards' spirituality in the *Narrative* is largely *contemplative* in its focus. Traditionally scholars have argued that Puritan spirituality was, in the main, more active in nature with an emphasis on deeds of charity and generosity and a life that would facilitate them. Not so much solitary prayer, but corporate and family worship was the highest expression of Puritan spirituality. This view is being increasingly challenged as our knowledge of Puritan life increases. Edwards rarely if ever speaks of concrete acts of compassion or love toward others. This isn't to say he would have opposed them. In fact, his life and pastoral ministry bear witness to a man who, although remarkably intellectual, cared deeply for the sheep entrusted to his care. I simply have in view his primary focus in the *Personal Narrative*. Countless sermons and other exhortations by Edwards refer to the necessity of mercy and love toward those in need.

Second, a primary difference between Edwards and Puritanism in general is his failure to endorse a specific "morphology" of conversion in which humiliation or conviction of sin is a necessary prelude to consolation and assurance. Edwards' most explicit confessions of sin and struggle for repentance came *after* his conversion, only as he progressively grew in the knowledge of the beauty and sweetness of Christ.

He was obviously more concerned with the *nature* of one's spiritual experience than with its *order* or *sequence* (something we saw earlier in the *Affections*). This may be why he says little in the *Personal Narrative* of his experience before the "new sense" and thus does not portray his life as do most evangelicals in terms of "before" and "after" conversion.

Third, there is an absence from the *Narrative* of any meaningful reference to historical or social context. On occasion he mentions where he was when an experience occurred, but in each case it is tangential to the experience itself. Little is said of family, friends, or intellectual interests (although the latter were massive!). As McClymond has said, "The *Personal Narrative* has no real plotline; it is less a genuine story than a depiction of successive states of experience."[7]

Fourth, one can hardly miss Edwards' emphasis on the benefits of *solitude* (in the *Affections* you may recall that he used the synonymous term "retirement"). Beyond the prayer booth that he built with his

[7]Ibid., 42.

childhood friends, he wrote of "particular secret places of my own in the woods, where I used to retire by myself." He speaks of wanting to be "alone in the mountains, or some solitary wilderness, far from all mankind, sweetly conversing with Christ." He spoke of "often walking alone in the woods and solitary places, for meditation, soliloquy, and prayer." When he wrote of then thirteen-year-old Sarah Pierpont (who would become his wife), he praised her for loving "to be alone, walking in the fields and groves," for she seemed "to have some one invisible always conversing with her."

Fifth, Edwards places great emphasis on personal *asceticism,* believing that his spiritual growth is directly related to his physical health and energy. McClymond points out that "one searches his writings in vain for any passage in which he expressed an unalloyed delight in any sort of physical activity."[8]

Self-examination or self-scrutiny is engaged only insofar as it reveals how far short of biblical holiness one has fallen, only insofar as it awakens the soul to the need for more of forgiveness and divine grace.

A word of clarification is in order here, for Edwards was anything but a gnostic! His appreciation for nature, the physicality of creation, and the revelation of divine beauty therein is enough to silence that charge. It is true, however, that he had little if any appetite for what we today would consider "leisure" activities or hobbies or "mindless pleasures." His life was one of single-minded pursuit of the knowledge and experience of God. He rigorously monitored what he ate and drank in order to maximize his intellectual and physical efficiency. He vehemently resisted anything that threatened to diminish his power of concentration or distract his focus.

Sixth, the vocabulary of the *Narrative* is instructive. It is remarkably vivid in the way it portrays personal and subjective experiences. Consider, for example, the frequency of the following terms: "sense" (twenty-two times), "affection" or "affect" (sixteen times), "contemplation" or "meditation" (fifteen times), "delight" or "delightful" (twenty-four times), "pleasing" or "pleasant" (fifteen times), and most significant of all, "sweet" or "sweetness" or "sweetly" (fifty-seven times)! Clearly, God was not a being merely to be known but a *person to be enjoyed!*

---

[8] Ibid., 44.

Seventh, Edwards spoke often of his frustration with mundane and temporal affairs of life, for they distracted him and detracted from the time and energy he might otherwise devote to contemplating God. In fact, he speaks of his responsibilities at Yale as the reason for his spiritual decline. He longed for peace and stability to pursue God unhindered and unencumbered.

Eighth, although he valued his acquaintances, Edwards gave no indication that he worked hard at developing close intimate friendships. Be it noted, however, that Edwards' entire life was wrapped up in community: he served as a pastor for most of his adult life, he cherished his relationship with his wife and children, and he spoke of heaven as a world of love in which *the saints' great joy is the joy of other saints*.

Ninth, Edwards' view of the Song of Solomon is instructive. He adopted an interpretation according to which the bride is not the corporate church but the individual believer. He testifies that no book affected him quite like the Song.

Tenth, and finally, his spirituality was thoroughly theocentric. God is most pleased with us and glorified when we ponder his beauty, reflect with relish on the splendor of his personality, and contemplate with joyful celebration his sovereignty in all affairs of life and salvation.

For Edwards, "seeing" God—that is, the spiritual "perception" or "apprehension" of God in himself, through nature and as revealed in Scripture—together with the satisfaction of soul it produced, was *an end in itself*. It does not serve as a means to some higher aspiration. It is itself the pinnacle and the purpose for which we have been redeemed. God created all things so that his beauty and glory might be seen and known and appreciated and rejoiced in by his creatures. "Complete absorption in God, rapt enjoyment of the divine 'sweetness,' and forgetfulness of one's self—here in a nutshell is Edwards' spiritual ideal."[9]

The format of what follows is simple and straightforward. I cite virtually all of the *Narrative*, interspersed with brief pastoral observations that are designed to elucidate Edwards' thought and encourage us in our own pursuit of the heart of God. There are a few instances in which I lift a passage from one part of the *Narrative* and combine

---

[9]Ibid., 48.

it with another, due to the common theme they address. If you wish to read the entire *Narrative* in sequence, I refer you to the several sources in which it may be found (see note 2 in this chapter). Unlike my treatment of the *Religious Affections,* I have not altered the original text of the *Narrative* except for an occasional change in punctuation or spelling to facilitate ease of reading.

21

A NEW SENSE OF
THE HEART

THE *PERSONAL NARRATIVE* opens with Edwards' portrayal of his religious experience as a child. As you read, note well that, with the benefit of both hindsight and extensive pastoral experience, he became quite skeptical of whether there was any saving value in these early encounters. Edwards was always brutally and biblically honest in his evaluation of the nature of religious experience, a concern of his that reached its climax in the publication of *Religious Affections*. So let's begin:

> I had a variety of concerns and exercises about my soul from my childhood; but had two more remarkable seasons of awakening, before I met with that change by which I was brought to those new dispositions, and that new sense of things, that I have since had. The first time was when I was a boy, some years before I went to college, at a time of remarkable awakening in my father's congregation. I was then very much affected for months, and concerned about the things of religion, and my soul's salvation; and was abundant in duties. I used to pray five times a day in secret, and to spend much time in religious talk with other boys; and used to meet with them to pray together. I experienced I know not what kind of delight in religion. My mind was much engaged in it, and had much self-righteous pleasure; and it was my delight to abound in religious duties. I with some of my schoolmates joined together, and built a booth in a swamp, in a very retired spot, for a place of prayer. And besides, I had particular secret places of my own in the woods, where I used to retire by myself; and was from time to time much affected. My affec-

tions seemed to be lively and easily moved, and I seemed to be in my element when engaged in religious duties. And I am ready to think, many are deceived with such affections, and such a kind of delight as I then had in religion, and mistake it for grace.

But in process of time, my convictions and affections wore off; and I entirely lost all those affections and delights and left off secret prayer, at least as to any constant performance of it; and returned like a dog to his vomit, and went on in the ways of sin. Indeed I was at times very uneasy, especially towards the latter part of my time at college; when it pleased God to seize me with a pleurisy in which he brought me nigh to the grave, and shook me over the pit of hell. And yet, it was not long after my recovery, before I fell again into my old ways of sin. But God would not suffer me to go on with any quietness. I had great and violent inward struggles, till, after many conflicts with wicked inclinations, repeated resolutions, and bonds that I laid myself under by a kind of vows to God.

I was brought wholly to break off all former wicked ways, and all ways of known outward sin, and to apply myself to seek salvation, and practice many religious duties; but without that kind of affection and delight which I had formerly experienced. My concern now wrought more by inward struggles and conflicts, and self-reflections. . . . But yet, it seems to me, I sought after a miserable manner; which has made me sometimes since to question, whether ever it issued in that which was saving; being ready to doubt, whether such miserable seeking ever succeeded. I was indeed brought to seek salvation in a manner that I never was before; I felt a spirit to part with all things in the world, for an interest in Christ. My concern continued and prevailed, with many exercising thoughts and inwards struggles; but yet it never seemed to be proper to express that concern by the name of terror.

This is a stunning confession on Edwards' part and incredibly instructive for us today, especially if we are the sort who quickly conclude that any display of interest in spiritual or religious matters is evidence of the new birth. Observe that Edwards was "very much affected" with religious impulses and was "concerned about things of religion" and his own "salvation." He delighted in the fulfillment of "religious duties," especially prayer (his youthful habit was to pray, in secret, no less than five times a day). He testified to affections that were "lively and easily moved." Yet, he could bring himself to describe only a "self-righteous pleasure" in them.

Notwithstanding this remarkable confession, Edwards evidently doubted that this was the fruit of genuine salvation. "I am ready to think," said Edwards, "many are deceived with such affections, and such a kind of delight as I then had in religion, and mistake it for grace." Were ever more relevant words spoken to the church of the twenty-first century? A person raises a hand, signs a card, walks an aisle, serves in the nursery, attends a prayer meeting, shares a "conversion" story, and we immediately assume they are saved, notwithstanding the fact that, as in Edwards' own case, they "return as a dog to its vomit" and continue on "in the ways of sin."

Was Edwards the boy truly converted? Perhaps, but my sense is that he thinks not. In words that he would later pen for the *Religious Affections,* these experiences proved *nothing* as to the nature of his relationship with God. They were not infallible "signs" of the Spirit's presence, but were the sort that are often found in those who later fall away and show themselves unregenerate.

The key words in these opening paragraphs of the *Narrative* are found where he refers to "that change by which I was brought to those new dispositions, and that new sense of things." He clearly has in mind here what he would later describe as "the new sense of the heart" that is the fruit of "a divine and supernatural light" that God in grace shines into the souls of his elect. Edwards will say considerably more about this in the remainder of the *Narrative,* but it is enough now to note that what so often passes for genuine conversion in our churches and revival meetings is little more than self-righteous pleasure in the external duties of religion, a sort of psychological pacifying of spiritual rumblings in the soul. Edwards' description of what he is convinced was his conversion experience follows below.

The Sovereignty of God: From Struggle to Sweetness

Edwards was born and reared in a Puritan society and family where the Reformed faith was defended with vigor. But one should not assume from this that Edwards himself always embraced this perspective on Christianity. Although he is known to history, and rightly so, as a relentless proponent of what is known as Calvinism, he was not always so. In these paragraphs from early in the *Narrative* he describes his struggle and the transformation that occurred:

From my childhood up, my mind had been full of objections against
the doctrine of God's sovereignty, in choosing whom he would to
eternal life, and rejecting whom he pleased; leaving them eternally to
perish, and be everlastingly tormented in hell. It used to appear like
a horrible doctrine to me.[1]

But I remember the time very well when I seemed to be convinced,
and fully satisfied, as to this sovereignty of God, and his justice in
thus eternally disposing of men, according to his sovereign pleasure.
But never could give an account, how, or by what means, I was thus
convinced, not in the least imagining at the time, nor a long time after,
that there was any extraordinary influence of God's Spirit in it; but
only that now I saw further, and my reason apprehended the justice
and reasonableness of it. However, my mind rested in it; and it put an
end to all those cavils and objections. And there has been a wonderful
alteration in my mind, in respect to the doctrine of God's sovereignty,
from that day to this; so that I scarce[ly] ever have found so much
as the rising of an objection against it, in the most absolute sense, in
God's showing mercy to whom he will show mercy, and hardening
whom he will. God's absolute sovereignty and justice, with respect
to salvation and damnation, is what my mind seems to rest assured
of, as much as of any thing that I see with my eyes; at least it is so at
times. But I have often, since that first conviction, had quite another
kind of sense of God's sovereignty than I had then. I have often since
had not only a conviction, but *a delightful conviction*. The doctrine
has very often appeared exceeding[ly] pleasant, bright, and sweet.
Absolute sovereignty is what I love to ascribe to God. But my first
conviction was not so.

Immediately following these paragraphs is Edwards' description
of what many believe to be his conversion. However, as you read it
you may conclude that what he speaks of is simply the first conscious
remembrance of the "new sense" that flows from regeneration. How
much earlier the new birth may actually have occurred in his experience is hard to tell:

The first instance that I remember of that sort of inward, sweet
delight in God and divine things that I have lived much in since, was
on reading those words, I Tim. 1:17. '*Now unto the King eternal,*

[1]I'm sure there are many reading Edwards' comments who would echo his sentiments. Divine
sovereignty in the salvation of sinners often strikes the soul as unfair and unjust, indeed, "a horrible
doctrine." It isn't my purpose to address the topic of divine election at this point, so I will simply refer
you to my book *Chosen for Life: The Case for Divine Election* (Wheaton, Ill.: Crossway, 2007).

immortal, invisible, the only wise God, be honour and glory for ever and ever, Amen.' As I read the words, there came into my soul, and was as it were diffused through it, a sense of the glory of the Divine Being; a new sense, quite different from any thing I ever experienced before. Never any words of Scripture seemed to me as these words did. I thought with myself, how excellent a Being that was, and how happy I should be, if I might enjoy that God, and be rapt up to him in heaven, and be as it were swallowed up in him for ever! I kept saying, and as it were singing over these words of Scripture to myself; and went to pray to God that I might enjoy him, and prayed in a manner quite different from what I used to do; with a new sort of affection. But it never came into my thought, that there was any thing spiritual, or of a saving nature in this.

From about that time, I began to have a new kind of apprehensions and ideas of Christ, and the work of redemption, and the glorious way of salvation by him. An inward, sweet sense of these things, at times, came into my heart; and my soul was led away in pleasant views and contemplations of them. And my mind was greatly engaged to spend my time in reading and meditating on Christ, on the beauty and excellency of his person, and the lovely way of salvation by free grace in him. I found no books so delightful to me, as those that treated of these subjects. Those words Cant. 2:1, used to be abundantly with me, I *am the Rose of Sharon, and the Lilly of the valleys.* The words seemed to me, sweetly to represent the loveliness and beauty of Jesus Christ. The whole book of Canticles [i.e., Song of Solomon] used to be pleasant to me, and I used to be much in reading it, about that time; and found, from time to time, an inward sweetness, that would carry me away, in my contemplations. This I know not how to express otherwise, than by a calm, sweet abstraction of soul from all the concerns of this world; and sometimes a kind of vision, or fixed ideas and imaginations, of being alone in the mountains, or some solitary wilderness, far from all mankind, sweetly conversing with Christ, and wrapt and swallowed up in God. The sense I had of divine things, would often of a sudden kindle up, as it were, a sweet burning in my heart; an ardor of soul that I know not how to express.

This is nothing short of breathtaking! Again, what Edwards has in mind is that impartation of "a divine and supernatural light" which accounts for "a new sense" of the glory and beauty and sweetness of the Divine Being. By the way, did you notice how often Edwards speaks of God and the knowledge of him in Christ as being "sweet"? Seven times in these two paragraphs he uses the adjective "sweet" or some form of it. This word will appear literally dozens of times in the remainder of the *Narrative*.

What Edwards wants us to grasp is that merely "understanding" God or "knowing" things "about" God is far and away different from that "sweet sense" of the divine glory, in which the soul relishes and rejoices in what the mind perceives. As Edwards would later write in his famous sermon, "A Divine and Supernatural Light," "There is a difference between having a rational judgment that honey is sweet, and having a *sense* of its sweetness."[2]

When he speaks of the "divine and supernatural light" he does not refer to the conviction of sin that unregenerate people experience. The Spirit can act upon the soul of the unregenerate without communicating himself to or uniting himself with that person. Nor is it to be identified with "impressions" made upon the "imagination." It has nothing to do with seeing anything with one's physical eyes. The divine and supernatural light does not suggest or impart new truths or ideas not already found in the written Word of God. It "only gives a due apprehension of those things that are taught in the Word of God." It is not to be identified with those occasions when the unregenerate are deeply and profoundly affected by religious ideas (as was Edwards in his youth). One may be moved or stirred or emotionally impacted by a religious phenomenon without believing it to be true. One need only think of the popular reaction to Mel Gibson's *The Passion* when it was first released.

What, then, is the "divine and supernatural light"? It is "*a true sense of the divine excellency of the things revealed in the Word of God, and a conviction of the truth and reality of them, thence arising.*"[3] A person doesn't "merely rationally believe that God is glorious, but he has a sense of the gloriousness of God in his heart."[4]

But what is the difference between "rationally" believing that God is glorious and having a "sense of the excellency" of God's glory? It is the difference between knowing that God is holy and having a "sense of

[2]Jonathan Edwards, "A Divine and Supernatural Light," in *A Jonathan Edwards Reader*, ed. John E. Smith, Harry S. Stout, and Kenneth P. Minkema (New Haven, Conn.: Yale University Press, 1995), 112.
[3]Ibid., 111, emphasis mine.
[4]Ibid.

the *loveliness"* of God's holiness. It is not only a "speculatively judging that God is gracious" but also "a sense how amiable God is upon that account" or sensing the "beauty" of God's grace and holiness.

Edwards bases this distinction on the difference between *two ways of knowing.* On the one hand, there is what he calls merely speculative, notional, cognitive awareness of some truth. On the other hand, there is "the sense of the heart" in which one *recognizes* the beauty or amiableness or sweetness of that truth and *feels pleasure and delight* in it. It is the difference between *knowing* or believing that God is holy and having a *sense* of or *enjoying* his holiness. Again, in language that appears also in the *Affections,* "There is a difference between having a rational judgment that honey is sweet, and having a sense of its sweetness."[5] Or yet again, "When the heart is sensible of the beauty and amiableness of a thing, *it necessarily feels pleasure in the apprehension.*"[6]

This new sense can come about indirectly when enmity in the soul is removed and the mind is enabled to focus and think and concentrate with more intensity on what is known. But it comes about directly when this divine and supernatural light enables the mind and heart, by "a kind of intuitive and immediate evidence," to be convinced of the truth of the superlative excellency of such things.

Anyone, even the unregenerate, can cognitively grasp the subject matter of Scripture. They can study it, analyze it, even memorize it, "but that due sense of the heart, wherein this light formally consists, is immediately [imparted] by the Spirit of God."[7] To mentally "see" the truth of Scripture is one thing, but *to spiritually "sense" its beauty and excellency and relish it as a treasure and prize of incomparable worth is possible only when the Spirit shines this great and glorious light of illumination into the human heart.* Said Edwards:

> Men have a great deal of pleasure in human knowledge, in studies of natural things; but this is nothing to that joy which arises from this divine light shining into the soul. This light gives a view of those things that are immensely the most exquisitely beautiful, and capable of delighting the eye of the understanding. This spiritual light is the dawning of the light of glory in the heart.[8]

---

[5]Ibid., 112.
[6]Ibid., emphasis mine.
[7]Ibid., 115.
[8]Ibid., 123.

This brief summation of "A Divine and Supernatural Light" has not been an unrelated theological digression from our consideration of the *Personal Narrative*. One cannot understand Edwards' narrative of his own conversion and spiritual journey apart from the truths he preached in this remarkable sermon.

22

VEHEMENT LONGINGS FOR GOD AND GODLINESS

Enjoying the Creator in the Creation

I've never been mistaken for an outdoorsman! My idea of "roughing it" is a weekend at a run-down Holiday Inn. But my appreciation for nature, indeed my delight in it, was initially awakened by the following comments of Edwards in his *Personal Narrative*.

George Claghorn, who edited the volume on Edwards' letters and personal writings for the Yale edition of his collected works, contends that "for Edwards, contemplation of nature took on a *sacramental* perspective."[1] That is to say, Edwards encountered the Creator in his creation. The physical, by divine design, has become a means or instrument by which we apprehend and appreciate the spiritual. The material realm, Edwards would argue, points beyond itself and reveals something of the nature and glory of its spiritual and creative origin. Or, to use the language of the apostle Paul, God's "invisible attributes, namely, his eternal power and divine nature, have been clearly perceived, ever since the creation of the world, in the things that have been made" (Rom. 1:20; cf. Ps. 19 and 104). So, read and enjoy!

> Not long after I first began to experience these things, I gave an account to my father of some things that had passed in my mind. I was pretty much affected by the discourse we had together; and when the discourse was ended, I walked abroad alone, in a solitary place in

---

[1]George S. Claghorn, introduction to "Personal Writings," in Jonathan Edwards, *Letters and Personal Writings*, ed. George S. Claghorn, vol. 16 of The Works of Jonathan Edwards (New Haven, Conn.: Yale University Press, 1998), 747, emphasis mine.

my father's pasture, for contemplation. And as I was walking there, and looking up on the sky and clouds, there came into my mind so sweet a sense of the glorious *majesty* and *grace* of God that I know not how to express. I seemed to see them both in a sweet conjunction; majesty and meekness joined together; it was a sweet, and gentle, and holy majesty, and also a majestic meekness; an awful sweetness; a high, and great, and holy gentleness.

After this my sense of divine things gradually increased, and became more and more lively, and had more of that inward sweetness. The appearance of every thing was altered; there seemed to be, as it were, a calm sweet cast, or appearance of divine glory, in almost every thing. God's excellency, his wisdom, his purity and love, seemed to appear in every thing; in the sun, moon, and stars; in the clouds, and blue sky; in the grass, flowers, trees; in the water, and all nature; which used greatly to fix my mind. I often used to sit and view the moon for a long time; and in the day, spent much time in viewing the clouds and sky, to behold the sweet glory of God in these things; in the mean time, singing forth, with a low voice my contemplations of the Creator and Redeemer. And scarce any thing, among all the works of nature, was so sweet to me as thunder and lightning; formerly, nothing had been so terrible to me. Before, I used to be uncommonly terrified with thunder, and to be struck with terror when I saw a thunderstorm rising; but now, on the contrary, it rejoiced me. I felt God, so to speak, at the first appearance of a thunderstorm; and used to take the opportunity, at such times, to fix myself in order to view the clouds, and see the lightnings play, and hear the majestic and awful voice of God's thunder, which oftentimes was exceedingly entertaining, leading me to sweet contemplations of my great and glorious God. While thus engaged, it always seemed natural to me to sing or chant forth my meditations; or, to speak my thoughts in soliloquies with a singing voice ["Sweet" or "sweetness" appears some nine times in these two paragraphs!].

Does nature affect you like that? Do you "see" God in the clouds and sky and grass and trees and rushing streams? Do thunder and lightning appear "sweet" to your soul, leading you to "sweet contemplations" of your great and glorious God? Edwards never viewed the natural creation as an end in itself. He would have considered it idolatry to derive delight from the complexity and design and grandeur of the physical realm were it not that such phenomena reflect and echo and embody the greatness and glory of their Creator.

No one has expressed this with greater clarity than John Piper. In his book *When I Don't Desire God*, he points us to Psalm 19:1ff. where we are told that "the heavens declare the glory of God, and the sky above proclaims his handiwork." Again, in Psalm 92:4 we read, "For you, O LORD, have made me glad by your work; at the works of your hands I sing for joy." Piper writes that he assumes "that this joy is not idolatrous—that is, I assume it does not terminate on the works themselves, but in and through them, rests on the glory of God himself. The works 'declare' the glory of God. They point. But the final ground of our joy is God himself."[2] Edwards would no doubt joyfully concur. Again, Piper writes:

> That is, we see the glory *of God*, not just the glory of the heavens. We don't just stand outside and analyze the natural world as a beam [of sunlight], but let the beam fall on the eyes of our heart, so that we see the source of the beauty—the original Beauty, God himself. . . . All of God's creation becomes a beam to be "looked along" or a sound to be "heard along" or a fragrance to be "smelled along" or a flavor to be "tasted along" or a touch to be "felt along." All our senses become partners with the eyes of the heart in perceiving the glory of God through the physical world.[3]

I'm still not nearly the outdoorsman I ought to be, but I'll never again gaze on a giraffe or a bug or a constellation or a cloud or a valley or a mountain stream or a bird in flight and fail to think of God and marvel at his power and worship him as the "Original" of all things beautiful.

Thirsting After God

Edwards made it clear in the *Affections* that, whereas true religion certainly consists of *more* than high and fervent affections, it cannot consist of *less*. That is to say, we are mistaken if we conclude that a person with great passion and longing and yearning for holiness and the knowledge of God is, by virtue of that *alone,* regenerate. Yet, a person who *is* regenerate will most assuredly pant after God and godliness, not unlike the desperation of a thirsty dear for the refreshing, life-giving waters of a desert oasis (see Ps. 42:1–2; 63:1).

---

[2]John Piper, *When I Don't Desire God: How to Fight for Joy* (Wheaton, Ill.: Crossway, 2005), 184.
[3]Ibid., 184–185. Piper's imagery of the beam of sunlight was based on a passage from C. S. Lewis (*God in the Dock* [Grand Rapids, Mich.: Eerdmans, 1970], 212).

In the following entry from the *Personal Narrative* we catch a glimpse of Edwards' own passion or "vehement longings" for God. Carefully read it, after which I'll make five brief comments:

> I felt then great satisfaction, as to my good state, but that did not content me. I had vehement longings of soul after God and Christ, and after more holiness, wherewith my heart seemed to be full, and ready to break; which often brought to my mind the words of the Psalmist, Ps. 119:28. *My soul breaketh for the longing it hath.* I often felt a mourning and lamenting in my heart, that I had not turned to God sooner, that I might have had more time to grow in grace. My mind was greatly fixed on divine things, almost perpetually in the contemplation of them. I spent most of my time in thinking of divine things, year after year; often walking alone in the woods, and solitary places, for meditation, soliloquy, and prayer, and conversation with God; and it was always my manner, at such times, to sing forth my contemplations. I was almost constantly in ejaculatory prayer, wherever I was. Prayer seemed to be natural to me, as the breath by which the inward burnings of my heart had vent.
>
> The delights which I now felt in the things of religion, were of an exceeding different kind from those before mentioned, that I had when a boy; and what I then had no more notion of, than one born blind has of pleasant and beautiful colors. They were of a more inward, pure, soul animating and refreshing nature. Those former delights never reached the heart; and did not arise from any sight of the divine excellency of the things of God; or any taste of the soul-satisfying and life-giving good there is in them.

First, I confess that I often feel "vehement longings" for the University of Oklahoma football team to win the national championship. I'm vehement in my longings for a good movie, a steak medium rare, and other comforts and conveniences that I'm convinced I can't live without. Why then am I not vehemently longing for the presence and glory and supremacy of Jesus? How is it that I have allowed my heart to be captivated by such lesser treasures? Why have I believed the lie that the pleasures they bring can fill my soul in a way that Jesus cannot? Oh, gracious Father, make known to me through your Spirit the beauty and majesty of Jesus that I might long for him, crave him, pursue him, and settle for nothing less than all that you are for me in him.

Second, do you find it interesting, as I do, that a Calvinist like Edwards would say, "I often felt a mourning and lamenting in my heart, that I had not turned to God sooner, that I might have had more time to grow in grace"? If God sovereignly determines when we turn to him in faith, how can Edwards lament that he did not turn to God sooner than he did?

Clearly, Edwards never permitted his confidence in divine sovereignty to undermine his moral accountability to do all that God commands. If Edwards did not turn to God before he did, only Edwards is to be blamed. The fault for human sin and willful resistance to the overtures of grace in the gospel lies with the human heart. Edwards never compromised his belief in the ultimate sovereignty of God in accomplishing his will. But he did not conduct his life by speculating on what may or may not be God's secret and decretive will. Nor did he sit passively waiting for some "divine seizure" to motivate, move, or compel him to obey. The rule for human behavior is the revealed or preceptive will of God which commands all men everywhere to repent. If Edwards did not repent before he did, only he was to blame.

Only you and I are at fault for failing to embrace the good news of the gospel before we did. If you struggle to reconcile these twin truths, don't. Identify in Scripture what you are called to do, confess your reliance on divine grace for all good things, and then "work out your own salvation with fear and trembling," knowing that "it is God who works in you, both to will and to work for his good pleasure" (Phil. 2:12–13).

Third, how does the human soul come to savor the sweetness of Christ Jesus? Only by seeing him, only by fixing the eyes of the heart on the revelation of him in the Word and the world (creation). Edwards was entranced with the beauty of Jesus because his "mind was greatly fixed on divine things; almost perpetually in the contemplation of them." This doesn't come easily, especially in a world that demands so much of our time and attention. Edwards was deliberate and resolute in his determination to spend time alone with God. He did it by spending every possible moment "in thinking of divine things, year after year; often walking alone in the woods, and solitary places, for meditation, soliloquy, and prayer, and conversation with God."

Fourth, Edwards walked and talked with God as with a friend, vocalizing the sighs of his soul, giving vent in prayer, often brief but always poignant. Oh, how God longs for this time with us. Do you know how passionate God is for your undivided devotion, to hear every cry, every need, however small or great? He will never turn you away!

Finally, do you feel "delight" in the things of religion, as did Edwards? Or are they a burden, an intrusion into a life preoccupied with stuff and still more stuff? Here Edwards hints that the pleasure he felt in religious duties as a boy was not saving in nature. Listen again: "Those former delights [from his youth] never reached the heart; and did not arise from any sight of the divine excellency of the things of God; or any taste of the soul-satisfying and life-giving good there is in them."

Does your pursuit of God arise from an awareness and relishing of his excellency, or from an anticipation of the favors and gifts you hope he will bestow? Oh, dear friend, there is "soul-satisfying and life-giving good" in God and nowhere else. He is the gospel.[4] He is the good news. Knowing him is what the mind was made for. Loving him is what the heart was made for. Being the temple of his abiding presence is what the body was made for.

Oh, God, we plead for your Spirit to stir within our selfish and worldly hearts those vehement longings for your Son, that we might see him in his glory, smell the sweet fragrance of his presence, and rest secure in the loving embrace of his arms. May we, in knowing and prizing and praising him, be forever ruined for anything else!

The Love of Holiness

In the previous citation Edwards spoke of "vehement longings of soul after God and Christ, and after more *holiness.*" What is your reaction on hearing the word "holiness"? Is its sound sweet and precious to you? Or does it conjure up images of a stern and inflexible God and a strict and joyless life?

During the nineteenth century the National Holiness Movement labored for a return to the vibrancy and passion of John Wesley and the depth of commitment so evident in the original Methodist movement. Sadly, they were not always successful. Their version of "holi-

---

[4]See John Piper, *God Is the Gospel* (Wheaton, Ill.: Crossway, 2005).

ness" often degenerated into a hideous form of legalism in which one's maturity was measured by the number of activities from which one abstained. Whereas many in the holiness movement were godly and yearned for Christ-like righteousness, others defined holiness as abstinence. On their list of taboos: the theater, ball games, playing cards, dancing, lipstick, tobacco, alcohol, all forms of female makeup, the curling or coloring of one's hair, neckties for men, Coca Cola, chewing gum, rings, bracelets or any form of worldly "ornamentation," and so forth. One was prohibited from attending a county fair or lodge meetings, or being involved in political parties or labor unions. Life insurance was seen as a lack of faith in God, and medicine was generally viewed as poison. How tragic!

Jonathan Edwards' perspective on holiness is stunning. It shouldn't be. It says something about how far removed we are from the biblical vision of holiness that we are surprised by his comments, that we find them so rare and unique and refreshing. Like the psalmist, he cherished the laws and precepts and commandments of God more than silver and gold (see Psalm 119). He speaks of a "longing" and "eager thirsting" and "earnest pressing after" the "blessed rules of the gospel."

Why do we find it odd that someone would feel such passion for authentic holiness? Edwards spoke of continual self-examination and "diligence" and "earnestness" in the pursuit of a holiness that he envisioned as "ravishingly lovely" and "amiable." Why? For one simple reason: he knew that God would never command or require anything that was harmful to his children. He knew that God's rules were the expression of a heart that sought nothing but good for those who fear him.

God's aim in all his commandments is our joy in Jesus. He prohibits nothing except what tends to diminish that joy. He commands nothing save what enhances that joy. Biblical laws and requirements and warnings exist solely to protect us from what will ultimately undermine our satisfaction in God's Son. They have been given not to deprive us of joy but to deepen it, not to inhibit our souls from experiencing eternal pleasures but to intensify and expand our capacity to see and taste and feel and sense the beauty and splendor of Jesus.

So keep reading these excerpts from Edwards' *Personal Narrative*. But read with a prayer that such passion for purity would be yours, that

God might awaken in your soul a hunger for holiness and a desire, as
Edwards says, to be "conformed to the blessed image of Christ":

> My sense of divine things seemed gradually to increase, until I went
> to preach at New York, which was about a year and a half after they
> began; and while I was there, I felt them, very sensibly, in a much
> higher degree than I had done before. My longings after God and
> holiness, were much increased. Pure and humble, holy and heavenly,
> Christianity appeared exceedingly amiable to me. I felt a burning
> desire to be in every thing a complete Christian; and conformed to
> the blessed image of Christ; and that I might live, in all things, accord-
> ing to the pure, sweet and blessed rules of the gospel. I had an eager
> thirsting after progress in these things, which put me upon pursuing
> and pressing after them.
>
> It was my continual strife day and night, and constant inquiry,
> how I should be more holy, and live more holily, and more becoming
> a child of God, and a disciple of Christ. I now sought an increase of
> grace and holiness, and a holy life, with much more earnestness, than
> ever I sought grace before I had it. I used to be continually examining
> myself, and studying and contriving for likely ways and means, how
> I should live holily, with far greater diligence and earnestness, than
> ever I pursued any thing in my life; but yet with too great a depen-
> dence on my own strength, which afterwards proved a great damage
> to me. My experience had not then taught me, as it has done since,
> my extreme feebleness and impotence, every manner of way; and the
> bottomless depths of secret corruption and deceit there was in my
> heart. However, I went on with my eager pursuit after more holiness,
> and conformity to Christ. . . .
>
> I remember the thoughts I used then to have of holiness; and said
> sometimes to myself, "I do certainly know that I love holiness, such
> as the gospel prescribes." It appeared to me that there was nothing in
> it but what was ravishingly lovely; and highest beauty and amiable-
> ness, a divine beauty, far purer than any thing here upon earth; and
> that every thing else was like mire and defilement, in comparison
> with it.
>
> Holiness, as I then wrote down some of my contemplations on
> it, appeared to me to be of a sweet, pleasant, charming, serene, calm
> nature, which brought an inexpressible purity, brightness, peaceful-
> ness and ravishment to the soul. In other words, that it made the soul
> like a field or garden of God, with all manner of pleasant flowers; all
> pleasant, delightful, and undisturbed; enjoying a sweet calm, and the

gently vivifying beams of the sun. The soul of a true Christian, as I
then wrote my meditations, appeared like such a little white flower
as we see in the spring of the years; low and humble on the ground,
opening its bosom to receive the pleasant beams of the sun's glory,
rejoicing as it were in a calm rapture; diffusing around a sweet fragrance; standing peacefully and lovingly, in the midst of other flowers
round about; all in like manner opening their bosoms, to drink in the
light of the sun.

There was no part of creature holiness that I had so great a sense
of its loveliness, as humility, brokenness of heart and poverty of spirit;
and there was nothing that I so earnestly longed for. My heart panted
after this, to lie low before God, as in the dust; that I might be nothing, and that God might be all, that I might become as a little child.

23

HEAVEN AND EARTH

"THE HEAVEN I DESIRED," wrote Edwards, "was a heaven of holiness; to be with God, and to spend my eternity in divine love, and holy communion with Christ. My mind was very much taken up with contemplations on heaven, and the enjoyments there; and living there in perfect holiness, humility and love. And it used at that time to appear a great part of the happiness of heaven, that there the saints could express their love to Christ. It appeared to me a great clog and burden, that what I felt within, I could not express as I desired. The inward ardor of my soul, seemed to be hindered and pent up, and could not freely flame out as it would. I used often to think, how in heaven this principle should freely and fully vent and express itself. Heaven appeared exceedingly delightful, as a world of love; and that all happiness consisted in living in pure, humble, heavenly, divine love."

I know what Edwards meant when he expressed his frustration in not being able to "freely and fully vent and express" his love for Christ. Physical pains hold us back. Relational struggles distract our thoughts. Fatigue limits how long we can praise him. Fleshly impulses defile even our highest and most sincere declarations of love. This is one reason why heaven is so appealing and the anticipation of it so spiritually animating. One day, and forevermore, we will pray and praise and celebrate and rejoice and enjoy God without the slightest tinge of lust or greed or pride or weakness or boredom. Even so, come Lord Jesus!

Edwards mentions, in passing, a time of pressure and emotional burden that weighed heavily on his soul, the remedy for which was "contemplations of the heavenly state." He continues:

It was a comfort to think of that state, where there is fullness of joy; where reigns heavenly, calm, and delightful love, without alloy; where there are continually the dearest expressions of this love; where is the enjoyment of the persons loved, without ever parting; where those persons who appear so lovely in this world, will really be inexpressibly more lovely, and full of love to us. And how sweetly will the mutual lovers join together, to sing the praises of God and the Lamb! How will it fill us with joy to think that this enjoyment, these sweet exercises, will never cease, but will last to all eternity.

How do you comfort your soul when life is bad or a bore? Is it with thoughts of an eternity where joy is "full" and undiminished? When you struggle to like, much less love, a brother or sister in Christ, do you strengthen your resolve to bless them with thoughts that a day is coming that will bring "the enjoyment of the persons loved, without ever parting"? Even those in this world whom we do love will in that world "really be inexpressibly more lovely and full of love to us." Better still, all of us who then will perfectly love one another will together, in perfect harmony of heart and voice, sing praises to God and the Lamb.

Perhaps Edwards' greatest insight into the glory of heaven is that "this enjoyment, these sweet exercises, will never cease, but will last to all eternity." But more than that, as Edwards makes clear in other writings, our enjoyment of heaven will actually increase and intensify and expand![1] Whatever joy we experience in heaven will forever grow. Whatever pleasures we feel will forever deepen. We will never fully and finally arrive, as if once we have tasted such sweet delights we will have exhausted their capacity to satisfy our souls. It will only get better, forever. It will only taste sweeter, forever. It will only appear more beautiful, forever. With each joyful encounter we will have touched only a small measure of an even greater, perpetual, infinite, and eternal increase!

What this means, quite simply, yet profoundly, is that *glorification never ends!* There is an instantaneous dimension to glorification, insofar as we will in a moment, in the twinkling of an eye, be changed from corruptible to incorruptible. Mortality will be forever swallowed up

[1]For a complete listing of the many sermons and miscellany entries where Edwards addresses this point, see the essay by Paul Ramsey, "Heaven Is a Progressive State," in Jonathan Edwards, *Ethical Writings*, ed. Paul Ramsey, vol. 8 of The Works of Jonathan Edwards (New Haven, Conn.: Yale University Press, 1989), 706–738.

in immortality. Weakness will give way to strength, disease to eternal healing, weariness to everlasting energy! So, too, will our souls experience this irreversible renewal. No longer will we feel the propensity to sin. Never again must we fight and struggle to resist the promptings of the flesh. For never so much as a nanosecond in the ages to come will God's people ever feel the force or magnetic appeal of a temptation to lust or greed or envy or pride or unbelief.

But glorification is more than *irreversible*. Yes, it is certainly that, insofar as we will never revert to our former ways. The energy of unbelief and anger and immorality will have been instantly and irreversibly banished, having given way to a body, soul, and spirit that are conformed to that of Jesus himself. But this is not to say that the perfection we will then experience will be incapable of expansion and intensification.

To suggest that at the time of our glorification we will know all that can be known of God, or that our enjoyment of him will at some point reach a pinnacle or point of termination, is to misunderstand both God's nature and ours. That is to say, one would have to conclude that God is finite. To say that our knowledge and enjoyment of God are subject to measure, or that they can reach a point beyond which there is neither anything more to be known of him nor anything in him capable of eliciting more enjoyment, is to say that God is calculable rather than incalculable, that he is fathomable rather than unfathomable. To say such things is to place quantifiable boundaries around his being or to predicate limitations to his nature.

Once we assert both that God is infinite and that we are finite, we can no longer speak meaningfully of *comprehensive* comprehension. Yes, God has made himself *comprehensible*. He has graciously revealed himself to us and by his Spirit has enabled us to understand truly and accurately what he is like. But *true* knowledge will *never* be *total* knowledge. To suggest that at some time or in some way in the eternal state we will have exhausted the reservoir of truths about God or that we will have plumbed the depths of his divine nature is to predicate a power to us that is inconsistent both with our being creatures and his being the Creator.

Our knowledge of God will never be in error, but neither will it be exhaustive. God is, by definition, *inexhaustible*. Consider what this means for our experience of him in the eternal state. Growth in knowledge, or new and heretofore unseen insights into something, invariably yields a response of some sort, whether amazement, delight, disgust, love, hate, gratitude, etc. Such is surely the case with the progressive unfolding of God's character throughout the course of eternity. Such a disclosure must be *progressive* for the simple fact that *there is no limit or end to what is disclosed*. God cannot be conceived as imparting *all there is to know of himself* in one revelatory act, for the word "all" cannot be predicated of God. "All" means the complete and quantifiable amount, the sum total, if you will, of what can be said about God and thus known of God. But again, if God is infinite, one can never say everything that can be said about him nor can one know him to such an extent that nothing new or heretofore unseen is possible.

So, each fresh insight into the personality of God is necessarily accompanied by fresh joy and delight, always greater and more intense than any and all joy previously experienced. As God reveals yet more and more of his nature and ways throughout the course of eternity, our minds are, correspondingly, ever more filled, our hearts are, correspondingly, ever more overwhelmed. With each new disclosure of splendor, with each new revelation of beauty, our enjoyment of him deepens and our gratitude grows and our delight deepens.

No wonder that Edwards found strength and drew comfort in meditating on the glory of heaven to come! Can we do any less?

Consecration

Although profoundly heavenly minded, Jonathan Edwards was no less dedicated to a vibrant and fruitful life for God on the earth. He would never have considered using the former to justify laxity in the latter. Consider the following, where he describes the commitment and consecration of his life to God:

> On *January 12, 1723.* I made a solemn dedication of myself to God, and wrote it down; giving up myself, and all that I had to God; to be for the future, in no respect, my own; to act as one that had no right to himself, in any respect. And [I] solemnly vowed to take God for my whole portion and felicity, looking on nothing else as any part of my happiness, nor acting as if it were; and [to take] his law for the constant rule of my obedience: engaging to fight, with all my might,

against the world, the flesh, and the devil, to the end of my life. But I have reason to be infinitely humbled, when I consider, how much I have failed, of answering my obligation.

We live in a society where demanding one's "rights" has become something of a national pastime. I have a "right" to do with my body whatever I want. I have a "right" to conduct my sexual life however I please. I have a "right" not to be treated disrespectfully by others. And on and on it goes.

Edwards believed he had no "rights." Let's be clear about this. He's not talking about political rights or the right to an education or property rights, or any such thing. He's talking about his relationship with God (although Edwards would be the first to say that even these other so-called "rights" were a gift of grace to an undeserving soul). He has no "rights" in himself, no claim to autonomous freedom, as if he can arbitrarily determine what he will do with his body or his time or his mind or his talents or his money. God owns everything.

Edwards, like every believer, has been "bought with a price," the precious blood of Jesus, and has no claim to anything in himself or regarding himself. Neither he, nor we, have any "right" to look at whatever we please or think whatever we please or sleep with whomever we please or spend our money however we please or pursue whatever career or course in life suits our fancy.

We are each bondslaves of Jesus Christ. We are not the "lord" of our lives. He is. Paul said that "in him we live and move and have our being" (Acts 17:28). That is to say, whatever breath we breathe, Christ grants it, whatever movements we make, he energizes them, however long we live, he sustains and preserves us each moment of each day until such time as he calls us to himself.

What would life look like if we were to take this seriously, if we were to awaken each day conscious of the fact that the only reason we woke up at all is because God mercifully willed it so? My mind is not free to think whatever it wants nor my fingers to type whatever I please nor my eyes to read whatever they fall upon. Every fiber of my being—body, soul, and spirit—belongs to the Lord who loved me and gave himself for me.

The brief statement above, taken from Edwards' *Personal Narrative*, is but a summation of the longer declaration of personal resolve that is found in the entry to his diary, recorded on Saturday, January 12, 1723. Read it closely, prayerfully, and make it your own:

> In the morning. I have this day, solemnly renewed my baptismal covenant and self-dedication, which I renewed, when I was taken into the communion of the church. I have been before God, and have given myself, all that I am and have, to God; so that I am not, in any respect, my own. I can challenge no right in this understanding, this will, these affections, which are in me. Neither have I any right to this body, or any of its members: no right to this tongue, these hands, these feet; no right to these senses, these eyes, these ears, this smell, or this taste. I have given myself clear away, and have not retained any thing, as my own. I gave myself to God, in my baptism, and I have been this morning to him, and told him, that I gave myself *wholly* to him. I have given every power to him, so that for the future, I'll challenge no right in myself, in no respect whatever. I have expressly promised him, and I do now promise Almighty God, that by his grace, I will not.
>
> I have this morning told him, that I did take him for my whole portion and felicity, looking on nothing else, as any part of my happiness, nor acting as if it were; and [I did take] his Law, for the constant rule of my obedience; and would fight, with all my might, against the world, the flesh and the devil, to the end of my life; and that I did believe in Jesus Christ, and did receive him as a Prince and Savior; and that I would adhere to the faith and obedience of the Gospel, however hazardous and difficult the confession and practice of it may be; and that I did receive the blessed Spirit, as my Teacher, Sanctifier, and only Comforter, and cherish all his motions to enlighten, purify, confirm, comfort and assist me. This, I have done; and I pray God, for the sake of Christ, to look upon it as a self-dedication, and to receive me now, as entirely his own, and to deal with me, in all respects, as such, whether he afflicts me, or prospers me, or whatever he pleases to do with me, who am his.
>
> Now, henceforth, I am not to act, in any respect, as my own. I shall act as my own if I ever make use of any of my powers to any thing that is not to the glory of God, and do not make the glorifying of him my whole and entire business: [I shall act as my own] if I murmur in the least at affliction; if I grieve at the prosperity of others; if I am in any way uncharitable; if I am angry because of injuries; if I revenge them; if I do any thing purely to please myself, or if I avoid any thing

for the sake of my own ease; [I shall act as my own] if I omit any
thing, because it is great self-denial; if I trust to myself; if I take any
of the praise of any good that I do, or that God doth by me; or if I
am in any way proud.[2]

Your Kingdom Come!

The merging of the interests of heaven and earth is nowhere better
seen in Edwards than in his passion for the advancement and glory of
God's *kingdom*. He often testified to having read anything he could
lay his hands upon which reported of the advancement of Christ's
lordship over all peoples and nations and rulers. On two occasions in
the *Personal Narrative* he describes his concern for the progress of the
kingdom:

> I had great longings, for the advancement of Christ's kingdom in the
> world; and my secret prayer used to be, in great part, taken up in
> praying for it. If I heard the least hint, of any thing that happened,
> in any part of the world, that appeared, in some respect or other, to
> have a favorable aspect on the interests of Christ's kingdom, my soul
> eagerly catched at it [i.e., connected with it or responded to it favor-
> ably]; and it would much animate and refresh me. I used to be eager
> to read public newsletters, mainly for that end, to see if I could not
> find some news, favorable to the interest of religion in the world.
>
> I very frequently used to retire into a solitary place, on the banks
> of Hudson's River, at some distance from the city, for contemplation
> on divine things and secret converse with God, and had many sweet
> hours there. Sometimes Mr. Smith and I walked there together, to
> converse on the things of God; and our conversation used to turn
> much on the advancement of Christ's kingdom in the world, and
> the glorious things that God would accomplish for his church in the
> latter days. . . .
>
> My heart has been much on the advancement of Christ's king-
> dom in the world. The histories of the past advancement of Christ's
> kingdom have been sweet to me. When I have read histories of past
> ages, the pleasantest thing in all my reading has been to read of the
> kingdom of Christ being promoted. And when I have expected, in my
> reading, to come to any such thing, I have rejoiced in the prospect,
> all the way as I read. And my mind has been much entertained and

---

[2]Jonathan Edwards, "Diary," in *A Jonathan Edwards Reader*, ed. John E. Smith, Harry S. Stout,
and Kenneth P. Minkema (New Haven, Conn.: Yale University Press, 1995), 268.

delighted with the Scripture promises and prophecies, which relate to the future glorious advancement of Christ's kingdom upon earth.

Why was Edwards so captivated by the *earthly progress* of the Christian faith? Because he was passionate about the supremacy of Christ in all things in the lives of all people in every country. Edwards was no crass triumphalist. He didn't strut or boast or take pride in the cause of religion. He rejoiced in these reports because he heard in them the echo, "Jesus is Lord!" He saw in them evidence of the ever-increasing recognition on the part of men and women that Jesus alone is King, that Jesus alone is Ruler of the rulers of the earth.

Jesus instructed his disciples to pray in this way: "Your kingdom come, your will be done, on earth as it is in heaven" (Matt. 6:10). Edwards saw in this petition the demand that our hearts be riveted on the expansion of Christ's lordship over all the earth, over every life, over every molecule, atom, and quark.

Should we not then celebrate each time we hear of a newly converted soul, a renewed church, a law that is passed which respects life and purity and righteousness? Should we not then rejoice when evil is defeated and dictators deposed and the hungry are fed and the homeless are clothed? Should we not then praise God when the gospel is preached and injustice is righted and good is vindicated? Yes! Lord, let your kingdom come! Let your will be done!

Edwards on the "End Times"[3]

At no time did Edwards believe or preach that America would be either the focus or the locus of the coming millennium. Rather, he suggested that, at best, America may be where those intermittent revivals would occur that eventually would bring on the millennium, which was at least two hundred and fifty years away.

Edwards was generally pessimistic about the prospects for religion

---

[3]The most helpful and instructive treatment of Edwards' eschatology is found in Gerald R. McDermott's *One Holy and Happy Society: The Public Theology of Jonathan Edwards* (University Park: Pennsylvania State University Press, 1992). My brief explanation here is greatly dependent on McDermott's excellent work. There is also a helpful overview of Edwards' eschatological concerns in Stephen J. Stein's essay, "Eschatology," in *The Princeton Companion to Jonathan Edwards*, ed. Sang Hyun Lee (Princeton, N.J.: Princeton University Press, 2005), 226–242. Stein reminds us that "Jonathan Edwards never used the term 'eschatology' in his private reflections or in his public writings concerning the 'last things.' The word was not coined in English before the fifth decade of the nineteenth century" (226).

in America. If New England in general and Northampton in particular was a "city set upon a hill" for all to see, it was as a *negative* example of behavior to avoid, not a model for people to imitate. The only sense in which America was a "Christian" land was that Christianity was the established religion.

He regularly denounced the people of New England (Northampton, Massachusetts, in particular) as being on the verge of committing the unpardonable sin. He feared the ultimate destruction of America and spoke often of the continuous need for repentance. If there was a consistent theme in his sermons, it wasn't that America would play a crucial role in the coming millennial glory but that God's judgment on her for her sin was imminent. "That he was so relentless and ferocious in denouncing his countrymen's sins makes it more comprehensible, though perhaps no less defensible, why they should have banished him to a lonely frontier outpost for most of his last decade."[4]

Contrary to considerable scholarly opinion, Edwards did not believe that the millennium would be situated in America. His view of the millennium was international and global, such that he condemned all egoistic nationalism.

Edwards did believe that the millennium was the goal of redemptive history. It was the purpose toward which God in providential power was directing human affairs. It would be the culmination of all the ages of human history. He believed that his generation was standing on the threshold of the age that would precipitate the millennium. This preparatory age would last, he believed, for another two hundred and fifty years, the millennium itself beginning somewhere around the year 2000.

Much of the confusion concerning Edwards' beliefs about the millennium came from one statement in his *Some Thoughts Concerning the Revival* (1742), where he declared that "this work of God's Spirit [i.e., the revival, the Great Awakening], that is so extraordinarily and wonderful, is the dawning, or at least a prelude, of that glorious work of God, so often foretold in Scripture." He later said that this "glorious work of God . . . must be near."[5] But "that glorious work of God"

---

[4]McDermott, *One Holy and Happy Society*, 35.
[5]Jonathan Edwards, "Some Thoughts Concerning the Revival," in Jonathan Edwards, *The Great Awakening*, ed. C. C. Goen, vol. 4 of The Works of Jonathan Edwards (New Haven, Conn.: Yale University Press, 1972), 353.

was not a reference to the millennium itself but "to a long period of intermittent revival that would lead up to the millennium."[6]

As for the awakenings or revivals of the late 1730s and early 1740s, these were but "forerunners of those glorious times so often prophesied of in the Scripture, and that this was the first dawning of that light, and beginning of that work which, in the progress and issue of it, would at last bring on the church's latter-day glory."[7]

Edwards believed the millennium would last for approximately one thousand years, that it would be a period of absolute peace and stability until Satan was loosed to lead his final apostasy. After he was destroyed, the final judgment would ensue. The reign of Christ during the millennium would be "spiritual." Christ's body would remain in heaven (the biblical "second coming" not to occur until the close of the millennial age). Most instructive is that "in all of Edwards' descriptions of the long period of revivals and international tumults that were to precede the millennium . . . America was either absent, vilified, or given leadership by default."[8]

[6]McDermott, *One Holy and Happy Society,* 51.
[7]Jonathan Edwards, in a letter "To William McCulloch," in Goen, ed., *Great Awakening,* 560.
[8]McDermott, *One Holy and Happy Society,* 85.

24

SUFFERING AND THE SWEETNESS OF CHRIST

In September, 1725, I was taken ill at New Haven, and while endeavoring to go home to Windsor, was so ill at the North Village, that I could go no farther, where I lay sick, for about a quarter of a year. In this sickness, God was pleased to visit me again, with the sweet influences of his Spirit. My mind was greatly engaged there, on divine and pleasant contemplations, and longings of soul. I observed that those who watched with me would often be looking out wishfully for the morning; which brought to my mind those words of the Psalmist, and which my soul with delight made its own language, *My soul waiteth for the Lord, more than they that watch for the morning; I say, more than they that watch for the morning;* and when the light of day came in at the window, it refreshed my soul, from one morning to another. It seemed to be some image of the light of God's glory.

This may not immediately strike you as a profound statement, but I found several comments in it that are highly instructive.

First, note that Edwards refused to conclude from his sickness that God had abandoned him. Although he lay sick for almost three months, an especially difficult thing for a man who early in life resolved never to waste a minute's time, he looked through the illness for God's presence and purpose. "God was pleased to visit me again," he notes, "with the sweet influences of his Spirit." We don't know what Edwards had in mind by "sweet influences" of the Spirit, but the subsequent reference to the engagement of his "mind" would suggest that God enlightened and illumined his mind to grasp and savor and relish the promises of Scripture that are unaffected by human trial and suffering.

Second, even in illness Edwards was at work! He spent this time "greatly engaged" on "divine and pleasant contemplations" and "longings of soul." He meditated on the sweet truths of Scripture, turning them over and over in his mind, ruminating, musing, soaking his soul in the beauty of Christ revealed therein. But more than that, he spent his time in "longings of soul." Perhaps this is a reference to prayer. I suspect that he redeemed this season of physical weakness to strengthen and nurture and exercise the muscles of his soul, crying out to God for his presence, venting his heart's desire for a sense of God's power, testifying repeatedly, "You are my Lord; I have no good apart from you" (Ps. 16:2), and yet again, "Whom have I in heaven but you? And there is nothing on earth that I desire besides you. My flesh and my heart may fail, but God is the strength of my heart and my portion forever" (Ps. 73:25–26).

Third, I'm intrigued by Edwards' reference to the morning light that "came in at the window." It "refreshed my soul, . . . [and] seemed to be some image of the light of God's glory." Edwards believed that virtually everything in the natural realm was an "image" or "shadow" of some divine reality or truth or principle pertaining to God and his way of redemption. After all, in Edwards' theology, "the end of creation was God's communication of himself—and thereby of his glory—to the understanding and will of his creatures. The universe itself was part of that divine self-communication, an act performed every moment by the power of the sovereign God."[1]

For Edwards, there was hardly any color or shape or process or movement in nature that didn't in some way embody and express a spiritual truth. Edwards once wrote that he expected to be ridiculed as "a man of very fruitful brain and copious fancy" because he believed "that the whole universe, heaven and earth, air and seas, and the divine constitution and history of the holy Scriptures" was "full of images of divine things."[2]

When Edwards lay sick in bed, he looked each morning for the first appearance of light breaking through the window, for in it he saw "the light of God's glory" and his soul was "refreshed"! I fear we take

---

[1] "Editor's Introduction," in Jonathan Edwards, *Typological Writings*, ed. Wallace E. Anderson and Mason I. Lowance, Jr., with David Watters, vol. 11 of The Works of Jonathan Edwards (New Haven, Conn.: Yale University Press, 1993), 9.
[2] Cited in ibid., 7–8.

so much for granted and ignore the magnitude of God's revelation of himself in creation. How often do we pause long enough to behold his beauty and power in the little things of life, whether a beam of light or a thunder cloud or the effortless flight of a bald eagle? If not so much as a sparrow falls from the sky apart from the will of our heavenly Father, consider how pervasive must the revelation of his glory be in the most mundane of events and phenomena of the physical world.

The next time you are ill or weakened or perhaps perfectly healthy and lying quietly in bed, open your eyes to the presence of the Creator in creation. Who knows what may be found in a simple beam of light!

Savoring the Savior

"Since I came to this town [i.e., Northampton]," wrote Edwards,

> I have often had sweet complacency in God, in views of his glorious perfections and the excellency of Jesus Christ. God has appeared to me a glorious and lovely Being, chiefly on account of his holiness. The holiness of God has always appeared to me the most lovely of all his attributes. The doctrines of God's absolute sovereignty, and free grace, in showing mercy to whom he would show mercy; and man's absolute dependence on the operations of God's Holy Spirit, have very often appeared to me as sweet and glorious doctrines. These doctrines have been much my delight. God's sovereignty has ever appeared to me [to be a] great part of his glory. It has often been my delight to approach God, and adore him as a sovereign God, and ask sovereign mercy of him.
>
> I have loved the doctrines of the gospel; they have been to my soul like green pastures. The gospel has seemed to me the richest treasure; the treasure that I have most desired, and longed that it might dwell richly in me. The way of salvation by Christ has appeared, in a general way, glorious and excellent, most pleasant and most beautiful. It has often seemed to me, that it would in a great measure spoil heaven, to receive it in any other way.

There is one primary lesson I hope we can see in what Edwards writes here. It is that the revelation of God in Scripture and in the person and work of his Son, Jesus Christ, is more than something to be acknowledged as truth. True it is, for what hope can we find in falsehood? But it is not enough merely to say, "I believe the gospel is true." Demons believe the gospel is true, and their destiny is the lake of fire.

What we see in this passage from Edwards is once again his emphasis on the "new sense of the heart" in which the "truths" of Scripture, particularly the "truths" about God, are perceived as lovely, as sweet, as glorious and as excellent. There is a *sense* in the soul that relishes the truths of Scripture rather than merely conceding them. There is a *sense* in the soul that enjoys the beauty of God's holiness rather than merely acknowledging it as an attribute of his character.

Edwards chose his language carefully. The doctrine of God has been his "delight." These are "sweet and glorious doctrines." Such truths are more than merely rational and reasonable, such that correspond to reality and are consistent with Scripture. They are "the richest treasure; the treasure that I have most desired, and longed that it might dwell richly in me." The way God saves people by sovereign mercy in Christ strikes Edwards as "glorious and excellent, most pleasant and most beautiful."

For Edwards, conversion is certainly not less than belief. But it is a kind of belief in which the transcendent and glorious and beautiful quality of what is believed takes root in the soul. Saving faith is such that the soul "feels" and "senses" the beauty in what God has done. There is a holistic response in which the redeemed heart is drawn by strong desire and affection and longing for the "amiableness" of truth and then rests satisfied in the radiant brilliance of the light of the gospel. All other competing "lights" are dim by comparison. All other competing "pleasures" are vain and unfulfilling when measured against those that endure "forevermore" (Ps. 16:11).

The Beauty and Sufficiency of the Son

John Piper writes, "Sometimes what we need from the Bible is not the fulfillment of our dream[s], but the swallowing up of our failed dream[s] in the all-satisfying glory of Christ."[3] I'm convinced that the reason this doesn't resonate with many souls or sound very encouraging is because few really believe that Jesus Christ is all-satisfying in such a way that they confidently trust in him on a daily basis to do what sin cannot do.

Merely testifying that Jesus is our all-consuming passion, or declar-

---

[3]John Piper, *When I Don't Desire God: How to Fight for Joy* (Wheaton, Ill.: Crossway, 2004), 101.

ing, "I have no good apart from you" (Ps. 16:2), often doesn't translate into sin-killing confidence in his goodness and beauty and power and presence. We need more than verbal profession of Christ's glory. We need what Edwards repeatedly referred to as "the new sense of the heart" in which Christ's glory appears ineffably sweet and pleasant to the soul and does so with such intensity that all rival pleasures are soiled and sullied by comparison.

But savoring the Son of God comes only as we see the Son of God, not with physical eyes but with the eyes of faith (Eph. 1:18), as we concentrate our focus on him in Scripture and the majesty of his creative handiwork in the world around us. This is not a singular experience, a passing glance cast his way intermittently in hopes of a radical change that will turn sin sour in our souls. This sort of spiritually flippant, casual acquaintance with Jesus will prove powerless in the face of the magnetic and alluring appeal of sin.

What I have in mind is a life-long, daily determination to "set the LORD always before me" (Ps. 16:8). This is the resolve of the will, empowered by grace, to plead with God that he "turn my eyes from looking at worthless things" (Ps. 119:37) and enable me to rivet my soul, mind, and will on the splendor of his Son. Needless to say, this prayer of the psalmist is only as good as the practical steps we take to rid our homes and cars and lives and leisure hours of whatever "worthless things" now fill them.

I don't have any easy answers or ready-made formulas on how to do it successfully. But when I read Edwards I'm encouraged once again that yes, perhaps it can be done, with God's help. On two occasions in his *Personal Narrative*, Edwards describes his experience of the beauty of Christ. As you read, remember that these are the words of a man who labored to find time alone with God, a man whose mind was saturated with Scripture, a man who, at an early age, prioritized his life and the use of his time so as to eliminate, as much as humanly possible, distractions and diversions and those soul-sapping, spiritually enervating activities that threaten to anesthetize our minds and cloud our spiritual vision:

> It has often appeared to me delightful to be united to Christ; to have him for my head, and to be a member of his body; also to have Christ

for my teacher and prophet. I very often think with sweetness, and longings, and pantings of soul, of being a little child, taking hold of Christ, to be led by him through the wilderness of this world. That text, Matt. 18:3, has often been sweet to me, *except ye be converted and become as little children, etc.* I love to think of coming to Christ, to receive salvation of him, poor in spirit, and quite empty of self, humbly exalting him alone; cut off entirely from my own root, in order to grow into, and out of Christ; to have God in Christ to be all in all; and to live by faith in the Son of God, a life of humble, unfeigned confidence in him. That Scripture has often been sweet to me, Ps. 115:1, *Not unto us, O Lord, not unto us, but unto thy name give glory, for thy mercy, and for thy truth's sake.* And those words of Christ, Luke 10:21, *In that hour Jesus rejoiced in spirit, and said, I thank thee, O Father, Lord of heaven and earth, that thou hast hid these things from the wise and prudent, and hast revealed them unto babes: Even so, Father, for so it seemed good in thy sight.* That sovereignty of God which Christ rejoiced in, seemed to me worthy of such joy, and that rejoicing seemed to show the excellency of Christ and of what spirit he was. . . .

I have sometimes had a sense of the excellent fullness of Christ, and his meekness and suitableness as a Savior; whereby he has appeared to me, far above all, the chief of ten thousands. His blood and atonement have appeared sweet, and his righteousness sweet; which was always accompanied with ardency of spirit, and inward strugglings and breathings, and groanings that cannot be uttered, to be emptied of myself, and swallowed up in Christ.

Once, as I rode out into the woods for my health, in 1737, having alighted from my horse in a retired place, as my manner commonly has been, to walk for divine contemplation and prayer, I had a view that for me was extraordinary, of the glory of the Son of God, as Mediator between God and man, and his wonderful, great, full, pure and sweet grace and love, and meek and gentle condescension. This grace that appeared so calm and sweet, appeared also great above the heavens. The person of Christ appeared ineffably excellent with an excellency great enough to swallow up all thought and conception, which continued as near as I can judge, about an hour; which kept me the greater part of the time in a flood of tears, and weeping aloud. I felt an ardency of soul to be, what I know not otherwise how to express, emptied and annihilated; to lie in the dust, and to be full of Christ alone; to love him with a holy and pure love; to trust in him; to live upon him; to serve and follow him; and to be perfectly sanctified and made pure, with a divine and heavenly purity. I have, several other times, had views very much of the same nature, and which have had the same effects.

Spiritual Heartburn

Sometimes, only mentioning a single word caused my heart to burn within me; or only seeing the name of Christ, or the name of some attribute of God. And God has appeared glorious to me, on account of the Trinity. It has made me have exalting thoughts of God, that he subsists in three persons: Father, Son and Holy Ghost.

The sweetest joys and delights I have experienced have not been those that have arisen from a hope of my own good estate, but in a direct view of the glorious things of the gospel. When I enjoy this sweetness, it seems to carry me above the thoughts of my own estate. It seems at such times a loss that I cannot bear to take off my eye from the glorious, pleasant object I behold without me, to turn my eye in upon myself, and my own good estate.

I want to focus on the second remarkable paragraph. Let me begin with this statement: "The sweetest joys and delights I have experienced have not been those that have arisen from a hope of my own good estate; but in a direct view of the glorious things of the gospel."

I often tell people that I'm a "hedonist" because I believe it is impossible to desire pleasure too much. But I'm a "Christian hedonist" because I believe the pleasure we cannot desire too much is pleasure in God and all that he is for us in Jesus.[4] Edwards, contrary to what some have alleged, was undeniably a Christian hedonist! He was unavoidably passionate about his own joy and delight and pleasure. By the way, so are you. But note well: the sweetest joys and delights that Edwards experienced did not arise from a hope that his "own good estate" would improve. His "happiness," if I am allowed to use that word, was not suspended on the potential for an increase of wealth or personal comfort or the praise of his peers or physical health or any such thing.

When we are asked, "How are you doing?" we typically respond based on the condition of our "own good estate." That is, we take stock of our stocks, we consider our cash flow, we evaluate a variety of external and physical circumstances that seem to define our lives, and

---

[4]See John Piper, *Desiring God* (Sisters, Ore.: Multnomah, 2003).

then respond accordingly. Edwards is echoing Asaph in Psalm 73:25: "Whom have I in heaven but you? And there is nothing on earth that I desire besides you." That's an easy text to recite until the "things" on earth that we just declared we don't desire suddenly disappear or are stolen or disintegrate or elude our grasp. That's when we get honest and confess, "Okay, I'm sorry, God, but there are a few things I desire besides you. I like you, God, but I find that I like you more when those things I said I didn't desire are affordable and easy to come by."

Can we honestly say that the "glorious things of the gospel" (by which I think Edwards primarily means God himself as he is revealed in the face of Jesus) are the source of our "sweetest joys and delights"? Or is our capacity to enjoy the glorious things of the gospel suspended on the improvement of our "own good estate"?

Edwards continues by saying, "When I enjoy this sweetness, it seems to carry me above the thoughts of my own estate." This is what the Puritans referred to as the "expulsive" power of a new affection. Edwards declares that the enjoyment of God is so sweet, so satisfying, so utterly transcendent that "thoughts" of his "own estate" are left behind and below. All else is tarnished when compared to the radiant brilliance of God. All else is hazy when compared to the glorious clarity of knowing him. The fear of losing the conveniences that would enhance his "own estate" is trumped by the joy and sweetness and pleasure that can be found in God's presence, at his right hand (Ps. 16:11). The power to live unaffected by financial loss or physical pain comes not from denying the hunger in your soul for pleasure but from finding the fulfillment of such craving in the glory and beauty and presence of God (what the author of Hebrews referred to as a "better" and "abiding" possession [10:34])!

This is why Paul could declare that he was "sorrowful, yet always rejoicing" (2 Cor. 6:10). He wasn't anesthetized to earthly pain or disappointment, but neither was he enslaved to it. He was fully in touch with the reality of "wasting away" (2 Cor. 4:16) and the inescapable "affliction" (v. 17) that awaits us in this life. But he did "not lose heart" (v. 16) because his hope was fixed on "an eternal weight of glory beyond all comparison" (v. 17). This hope is fueled and energized when "we look not to the things that are seen but to the things that are unseen" (v. 18), or as Edwards put it, when we engage our souls "in a direct view of the glorious things of the gospel."

Finally, "It seems at such times a loss that I cannot bear," said Edwards, "to take off my eye from the glorious, pleasant object I behold without me, to turn my eye in upon myself, and my own good estate."

That "glorious, pleasant object" beyond ourselves is, of course, God! How painful, said Edwards, how unbearable the loss, when I turn my eye in upon myself and become obsessed with "my own good estate," whether that be the image I behold in a mirror, or the diversity of an investment portfolio, or whatever it is in life in the absence of which I cannot imagine being happy. Just think of it: being of such a mind that the only unbearable loss you can conceive is in failing to "see" the splendor and majesty of God in Christ!

25

WORD AND SPIRIT

Searching the Scriptures

Edwards' love affair with the Bible was passionate and long-standing. It was there that he beheld the beauty of Christ. The power of the living God was made known to him in its pages. The glory of the Spirit's abiding presence was awakened in his heart as he meditated on its majestic truths. There is one short passage in the *Narrative* where Edwards speaks of the transforming effect of Scripture on his life:

> I had then, and at other times, the greatest delight in the holy Scriptures, of any book whatsoever. Oftentimes in reading it, every word seemed to touch my heart. I felt a harmony between something in my heart, and those sweet and powerful words. I seemed often to see so much light exhibited by every sentence, and such a refreshing food communicated, that I could not get along in reading; often dwelling long on one sentence, to see the wonders contained in it; and yet almost every sentence seemed to be full of wonders.

How far removed this is from the declarations of boredom that I so often hear from people who describe their reaction to reading Scripture! Yet again, Edwards wrote of the power of Scripture to awaken and sustain life, and to bring a satisfaction to the human heart that no rival "letter" could touch:

> And I have sometimes had an affecting sense of the excellency of the word of God, as a word of life; as the light of life; a sweet, excellent life-giving word; accompanied with a thirsting after that word, that it might dwell richly in my heart.

I think what Edwards refers to must be what the author of Psalm 119 had in mind when he spoke repeatedly of the impact of Scripture on his soul. Consider the following brief sampling and ask yourself if such vivid and passionate language accurately portrays your attitude toward the glory and power of God's Word:

"In the way of your testimonies *I delight as much as in all riches*" (v. 14).

"*I will delight* in your statutes" (v. 16).

"*My soul is consumed with longing* for your rules at all times" (v. 20).

"Your testimonies are my *delight*" (v. 24).

"Behold, I *long* for your precepts" (v. 40).

"For I find my *delight* in your commandments, *which I love*" (v. 47).

"The law of your mouth is *better to me than thousands of gold and silver pieces*" (v. 72).

"*Oh how I love your law!*" (v. 97).

"How *sweet* are your words to my taste, *sweeter than honey to my mouth!*" (v. 103).

"Your testimonies are my heritage forever, for they are *the joy of my heart*" (v. 111).

"Therefore *I love your commandments above gold, above fine gold*" (v. 127).

"I *rejoice* at your word like one who finds great spoil" (v. 162).

"My soul keeps your testimonies; *I love them exceedingly*" (v. 167).

Do you dwell "long on one sentence" or skim quickly with only a cursory glance at words on a page? The greatest profit that I gain from Scripture is when I pause to take a word or phrase or sentence and turn it over and over again in my mind, speaking it aloud, perhaps even singing it unto the Lord. Memorize it. Muse on it. Ruminate. Reflect. Cry out to the Spirit for the light of understanding. Evaluate your soul and mind and life and leisure time in the light of its truth. Place your thoughts and deeds and desires and daydreams under its authority.

Those incredible statements from Psalm 119 should never be read in isolation from the rest of the psalm. The reason God's Word resonated with such sweet savor in the soul of the psalmist is because he was committed to seeking the Lord with his "whole heart" (Ps. 119:2, 10) and to meditating on his precepts (119:15) and to fixing his eyes on God's "ways" (119:15). His resolve was to "keep [God's] law continually, forever and ever" (119:44). Listen to the psalmist's prayer, repeated over and again:

"Open my eyes, that I may behold wondrous things out of your law" (v. 18).

"Teach me your statutes!" (vv. 26, 68, 124, 135).

"Make me understand the way of your precepts" (v. 27).

"Graciously teach me your law!" (v. 29).

"Teach me, O LORD, the way of your statutes" (v. 33).

"Give me understanding that I may learn your commandments" (v. 73; see also vv. 34, 125, 144, 169).

"Teach me good judgment and knowledge" (v. 66).

"Teach me your rules" (v. 108).

If this were our prayer, perhaps then, like Edwards, we would begin to feel "a harmony" between our hearts and "those sweet and powerful words" and to taste "a refreshing food" in God's Word and see the "wonders contained in it." Rest assured of this: God will not allow his Word to rest lightly on the heart of one who longs to experience its life-changing, sin-killing, Christ-exalting power.

Filled with the Spirit

Jonathan Edwards was a cessationist. Largely because of excessive and fanatical behavior associated with the First Great Awakening, he was concerned with the way in which certain people justified unwise, even unbiblical, decisions by appealing to having heard "the voice of God." He also opposed the contemporary validity of revelatory gifts (especially prophecy) because he believed, falsely in my opinion, that such would undermine the finality and sufficiency of Scripture. I mention this only to point out that, although I disagree with Edwards on this issue, his belief didn't diminish in the least his love and appreciation for the Holy Spirit.

Edwards' rather unique understanding of the Spirit is nowhere better seen than in his attempt to account for triunity in the Godhead. In a statement from his *Essay on the Trinity* he wrote the following:

> The Father is the deity subsisting in the prime, unoriginated and most absolute manner, or the deity in its direct existence. The Son is the deity generated by God's understanding, or having an idea of Himself and subsisting in that idea. The Holy Ghost is the deity subsisting in act, or the divine essence flowing out and breathed forth in God's infinite love to and delight in Himself. And . . . the whole Divine essence does truly and distinctly subsist both in the Divine idea and Divine love, and that each of them are properly distinct persons.[1]

Edwards is careful to insist that whereas the Spirit is the love and delight that eternally flows between the Father and the Son, he is not for that reason inferior to either, for "the *whole* Divine essence" truly subsists in him. All the attributes and glory of the divine nature are as eternally and equally present in the third person of the Godhead as in the first two. And lest someone suggest that this reduces the Spirit to an impersonal force passing between Father and Son, Edwards is again quick and insistent that "each of them," Father, Son, and Spirit, "are properly distinct *persons.*"

He also spoke and wrote often of the ministry of the Spirit, primarily in terms of the work of sanctification and illumination. Consider the following:

[1]Jonathan Edwards, "Essay on the Trinity," in *Treatise on Grace and Other Posthumously Published Writings,* ed. Paul Helm (Cambridge, Mass.: James Clarke, 1971), 118.

I have many times had a sense of the glory of the third person in the
Trinity, in his office of Sanctifier; in his holy operations, communicating divine light and life to the soul. God, in the communications of
his Holy Spirit, has appeared as an infinite fountain of divine glory
and sweetness; being full, and sufficient to fill and satisfy the soul;
pouring forth itself in sweet communications; like the sun in its glory,
sweetly and pleasantly diffusing light and life.

Here again we see Edwards' highly sensory language in describing
his perception of the nature and work of God. Like a self-replenishing
fountain that forever flows, God pours forth himself in "sweet communications." He is a measureless, incalculable reservoir of glory and
light, who, in making himself known and giving of himself to hell-
deserving sinners, suffers no loss, experiences no lack, and never, ever
runs dry! He is more than adequate and able to "fill and satisfy the
soul" of men and women who thirst for his presence.

Edwards' language is reminiscent of Paul's declaration in Acts
17:25 concerning the independent, all-sufficiency of God, who is not
"served by human hands, as though he needed anything, since he himself gives to all mankind life and breath and everything." If we truly
believe, as Edwards did, that God is "an infinite fountain of divine
glory and sweetness," we will not make the blasphemous mistake of
thinking that we, by our worship or offerings or activities or good
intentions, can in any way add to or supplement or support or increase
or enhance his glory and greatness.

So, if God is "an infinite fountain of divine glory and sweetness,"
how do we worship him? How do we honor him? With what attitude
and intent should we approach him? In what way do we "give" glory
to God without belittling him as needy and dependent on us? John
Piper tells us:

God has no needs that I [or anyone else] could ever be required to
satisfy. God has no deficiencies that I might be required to supply.
He is complete in himself. He is overflowing with happiness in the
fellowship of the Trinity. The upshot of this is that God is a mountain
spring, not a watering trough. A mountain spring is self-replenishing.
It constantly overflows and supplies others. But a watering trough
needs to be filled with a pump or bucket brigade. So if you want to
glorify the worth of a watering trough you work hard to keep it full

and useful. But if you want to glorify the worth of a spring you do it by getting down on your hands and knees and drinking to your heart's satisfaction, until you have the refreshment and strength to go back down in the valley and tell people what you've found. You do not glorify a mountain spring by dutifully hauling water up the path from the river below and dumping it in the spring. What we have seen is that God is like a mountain spring, not a watering trough. And since that is the way God *is*, we are not surprised to learn from Scripture—and our faith is strengthened to hold fast—that the way to *please* God is to come to him to get and not to give, to drink and not to water. He is most glorified in us when we are most satisfied in him.

My hope as a desperate sinner, who lives in a Death Valley desert of unrighteousness, hangs on this biblical truth: that God is the kind of God who will be pleased with the one thing I have to offer—my thirst. That is why the sovereign freedom and self-sufficiency of God are so precious to me: they are the foundation of my hope that God is delighted not by the resourcefulness of bucket brigades, but by the bending down of broken sinners to drink at the fountain of grace. . . .

In other words, this unspeakably good news for helpless sinners— that God delights not when we offer him our strength but when we wait for his—this good news that I need to hear so badly again and again, is based firmly on a vision of God as sovereign, self-sufficient and free.[2]

Here, then, is how we must come to God, whether to serve him or worship him or enjoy all that he is for us in Jesus:

Come, confessing your utter inability to do or offer anything that will empower God or enrich, enhance, or expand God.

Come, with heartfelt gratitude to God for the fact that whatever you own, whatever you are, whatever you have accomplished or hope to accomplish, is all from him, a gift of grace.

Come, declaring in your heart and aloud that if you serve, it is in the strength that God supplies (1 Pet. 4:10); if you give money, it is from the wealth God has enabled you to earn; if it is praise of who he is, it is from the salvation and knowledge of God that he himself has provided for you in Christ Jesus.

Come, declaring the all-sufficiency of God in meeting your every

---

[2]John Piper, *The Pleasures of God* (Portland, Ore.: Multnomah, 1991), 215–216.

need. Praise his love, because if he were not loving, you would be justly and eternally condemned. Praise his power, because if he were weak, you would have no hope that what he has promised he will fulfill. Praise his forgiving mercy, because apart from his gracious determination to wash you clean in the blood of Christ, you would still be in your sin and hopelessly lost. So, too, with every attribute, praise him!

Come, with an empty cup, happily pleading: "God, glorify yourself by filling it to overflowing!"

Come, with a weak and wandering heart, joyfully beseeching: "God, glorify yourself by strengthening me to do your will and remain faithful to your ways!"

Come, helpless, expectantly praying: "God, glorify yourself by delivering me from my enemies and troubles!"

Come, with your sin, gratefully asking: "God, glorify yourself by setting me free from bondage to my flesh and breaking the grip of lust and envy and greed in my life!"

Come, with your hunger for pleasure and joy, desperately crying: "God, glorify yourself by filling me with the fullness of joy! God, glorify yourself by granting me pleasures that never end! God, glorify yourself by satisfying my heart with yourself! God, glorify yourself by enthralling me with your beauty . . . by overwhelming me with your majesty . . . by taking my breath away with fresh insights into your incomparable and infinite grandeur! God, glorify yourself by shining into my mind the light of the knowledge of God in the face of Jesus Christ!"

26

A PAINFUL BUT PROFITABLE SENSE OF SIN

ONE SECTION IN EDWARDS' *Personal Narrative* has proved troubling to some Christians. They find Edwards' description of his own sinfulness to be excessively introspective, unduly pessimistic, and downright morbid. I've heard it said that we may justifiably view ourselves in this way *before* our conversion, but once we have been born again, justified, and forgiven, being as we are now new creatures in Christ, our perspective should take on a decidedly more positive tone. Here is Edwards' description:

> Often, since I lived in this town, I have had very affecting views of my own sinfulness and vileness; very frequently to such a degree as to hold me in a kind of loud weeping, sometimes for a considerable time together, so that I have often been forced to shut myself up. I have had a vastly greater sense of my own wickedness, and the badness of my heart, than ever I had before my conversion. It has often appeared to me, that if God should mark iniquity against me, I should appear the very worst of all mankind; of all that have been, since the beginning of the world to this time; and that I should have by far the lowest place in hell. When others, that have come to talk with me about their soul concerns, have expressed the sense they have had of their own wickedness, by saying that it seemed to them that they were as bad as the devil himself, I thought their expressions seemed exceeding faint and feeble, to represent my wickedness.
>
> My wickedness, as I am in myself, has long appeared to me perfectly ineffable, and swallowing up all thought and imagination; like an infinite deluge, or mountains over my head. I know not how to

express better, what my sins appear to me to be, than by heaping infinite upon infinite, and multiplying infinite by infinite. Very often, for these many years, these expressions are in my mind, and in my mouth, 'Infinite upon infinite! Infinite upon infinite!' When I look into my heart, and take a view of my wickedness, it looks like an abyss infinitely deeper than hell. And it appears to me, that were it not for free grace, exalted and raised up to the infinite height of all the fullness and glory of the great Jehovah, and the arm of his power and grace stretched forth in all the majesty of his power, and in all the glory of his sovereignty, I should appear sunk down in my sins below hell itself, far beyond the sight of every thing, but the eye of sovereign grace, that can pierce even down to such a depth. And yet it seems to me, that my conviction of sin is exceeding small, and faint; it is enough to amaze me, that I have no more sense of my sin. I know certainly that I have very little sense of my sinfulness. When I have had turns of weeping and crying for my sins, I thought I knew at the time that my repentance was nothing to my sin.

I have greatly longed of late for a broken heart, and to lie low before God; and, when I ask for humility, I cannot bear the thoughts of being no more humble than other Christians. It seems to me, that though their degrees of humility may be suitable for them, yet it would be a vile self-exaltation in me, not to be the lowest in humility of all mankind. Others speak of their longing to be 'humbled to the dust'; that may be a proper expression for them, but I always think of myself, that I ought, and it is an expression that has long been natural for me to use in prayer, "to lie infinitely low before God." And it is affecting to think, how ignorant I was, when a young Christian, of the bottomless, infinite depths of wickedness, pride, hypocrisy and deceit, left in my heart.

Does Edwards exaggerate his own sinfulness? Was he the victim of an overly-sensitive conscience? From our perspective, yes. From his, no. From all we know of his life, and we know a great deal, he was by common consensus one of the most godly men who ever lived. I don't think Edwards' conclusion concerning himself is the result of some quantitative comparative analysis, as if he literally measured his wickedness against that of all others. Yes, there are degrees of sin and evil among men. Some are more wicked than others. But Edwards, I suggest, is concerned only with how far short he falls from *God's* standard, not that of some other human.

Surely his sense of personal depravity is the fruit of seeing himself over against the infinite holiness of God. As far as Edwards was concerned, the only reasonable conclusion was that he was "the very worst" of all men, deserving of "the lowest place in hell." May I be so bold to suggest that if you and I have never come to a similar conclusion, we have spent too much time comparing ourselves to others rather than looking at our souls in the light of transcendent righteousness.

So what accounts for Edwards' vivid sense of personal depravity and wickedness? I suggest it comes from his knowledge of God. Perhaps we don't see ourselves this way because we don't see God at all. Or if we do see him, we see little of his holiness and the magnitude of his purity and the measureless sweep of his righteousness and the unimaginable depths of his integrity and the commitment of his will to the vindication of truth and goodness. For if we knew God as he is, what so easily and often passes for "minor indiscretions" in us would suddenly appear appallingly revolting and horrendously evil.

If you stand in the darkness, depravity is difficult to see. But when you walk in the light of God's glory, every spot and every stain is magnified beyond words. This is why Edwards felt what we don't. Might it also be that we've become so accustomed to our sin, indeed, comfortable with it, that its presence in our souls arouses little more than a whimper of conviction?

In our therapeutic, anthropocentric world, many would say to this Puritan, "Ease up, Jon! Don't be so hard on yourself. You're not nearly as bad as you think you are. You just need a little help with your self-image." I can only conclude that Edwards' description is not the result of what we today would call "low self-esteem," but comes from a biblically-informed "high God-esteem"!

Could this also be why Edwards had such a profound view of hell and its eternal torments and the justice of unending punishment? Resistance to the concept of hell is the direct result of ignorance of God. With the knowledge of God comes the awareness of sin. And with the awareness of sin, hell seems not so unreasonable. We minimize God and thus find the notion of hell unjust.

We must also remember that this sense of personal depravity was far from paralyzing to Edwards. It didn't cripple his determination to walk in purity. He refused to wallow in the reality of his own moral corruption or to use it as an excuse to give up on God or to justify a life given to passivity or, worse still, perversion. How so, you ask? Because the only thing that stood forth in his mind with greater clarity and power than the reality of sin was the vision of God's grace, unending love, and redemptive mercy in Christ Jesus. Hear him again: "Were it not for free grace, exalted and raised up to the infinite height of all the fullness and glory of the great Jehovah, and the arm of his power and grace stretched forth in all the majesty of his power, and in all the glory of his sovereignty, I should appear sunk down in my sins below hell itself; far beyond the sight of every thing, but the eye of sovereign grace, that can pierce even down to such a depth."

Ah! The "eye of sovereign grace"! It peers into the depths of the lowest hell and elevates the sunken, sinful soul to heights of joy and freedom and forgiveness.

Joyfully Dependent

As I said before, Edwards wasn't driven to despair by the reality of his own sin but was compelled to depend ever more urgently on the strong grace and sovereign good pleasure of God. He writes:

> I have a much greater sense of my universal, exceeding dependence on God's grace and strength, and mere good pleasure, of late, than I used formerly to have; and have experienced more of an abhorrence of my own righteousness. The very thought of any joy arising in me, on any consideration of my own amiableness, performances, or experiences, or any goodness of heart or life, is nauseous and detestable to me. And yet I am greatly afflicted with a proud and self-righteous spirit, much more sensibly than I used to be formerly. I see that serpent rising and putting forth its head continually, everywhere, all around me.

How strange such words sound in modern ears! When people today consider their deeds and what they imagine is their "goodness of heart or life," they strut. They strain to ensure that others take note of their achievements. For many, such joy is the aim of life. For Edwards, such joy is detestable, the source of a spiritual smugness that made him sick to his stomach.

Are we as aware as he of our "universal, exceeding dependence on

God's grace and strength, and mere good pleasure"? I doubt it. When I read Edwards' words I'm reminded of 2 Corinthians 1:8–11, where Paul describes how he was "so utterly burdened beyond . . . strength that [he] despaired of life itself" (v. 8b). He felt as if the "sentence of death" had been pronounced over him (v. 9a). But all this, he says, "was to make us rely not on ourselves but on God who raises the dead" (v. 9b).

James Denney, in his commentary on 2 Corinthians, captures the spirit of what Edwards has in view:

> It is natural . . . for us to trust in ourselves. It is so natural, and so confirmed by the habits of a lifetime, that no ordinary difficulties or perplexities avail to break us of it. It takes all God can do to root up our self-confidence. He must reduce us to despair; He must bring us to such an extremity that the one voice we have in our hearts, the one voice that cries to us wherever we look round for help, is death, death, death. It is out of this despair that the superhuman hope is born. It is out of this abject helplessness that the soul learns to look up with new trust to God. . . . How do most of us attain to any faith in Providence? Is it not by proving, through numberless experiments, that it is not in man that walketh to direct his steps? Is it not by coming, again and again, to the limit of our resources, and being compelled to feel that unless there is a wisdom and a love at work on our behalf, immeasurably wiser and more benign than our own, life is a moral chaos? . . . *Only desperation opens our eyes to God's love.*[1]

Concluding Comments on the Excellency of the Gospel

I find it fitting that Edwards would conclude his *Narrative* with the following observations on the excellency of the gospel itself.

> Though it seems to me that, in some respects, I was a far better Christian, for two or three years after my first conversion, than I am now; and lived in a more constant delight and pleasure; yet, of late years, I have had a more full and constant sense of the absolute sovereignty of God, and a delight in that sovereignty, and have had more of a sense of the glory of Christ, as a Mediator revealed in the

---

[1]James Denney, "The Second Epistle to the Corinthians," in W. Robertson Nicoll, ed., *The Expositor's Bible*, 6 vols. (New York: Wilbur B. Ketcham, n.d.), 5:724.

gospel. On one Saturday night, in particular, I had such a discovery of the excellency of the gospel above all other doctrines, that I could not but say to myself, "This is my chosen light, my chosen doctrine"; and of Christ, "This is my chosen Prophet." It appeared sweet, beyond all expression, to follow Christ, and to be taught, and enlightened, and instructed by him; to learn of him, and live to him.

Another Saturday night *(January 1739)* I had such a sense, how sweet and blessed a thing it was to walk in the way of duty; to do that which was right and meet to be done, and agreeable to the holy mind of God; that it caused me to break forth into a kind of loud weeping, which held me some time, so that I was forced to shut myself up, and fasten the doors. I could not but, as it were, cry out, "How happy are they which do that which is right in the sight of God! They are blessed indeed, they are the happy ones!" I had, at the same time, a very affecting sense, how meet and suitable it was that God should govern the world, and order all things according to his own pleasure; and I rejoiced in it, that God reigned, and that his will was done.

What moves you to tears? For some, I fear it is the prospect of biblical obedience. They cringe under what they believe is the oppressive burden of divine law. They feel hemmed in, as if confined by a biblical straitjacket. God appears to them as a grumpy despot who wants everyone to be as unhappy as he is. The commandments of his Word strike their souls as a deliberate strategy to deprive them of what little happiness and pleasure they've been able to achieve to this point in life. So, when they think of such words as "duty" and what is "right and meet to be done," they weep.

For Edwards, walking "in the way of duty" was so "sweet and blessed" that he broke forth in such "loud weeping" that he had to shut himself away lest he be a disturbance to others! Where did this perspective on Christian living come from? It came from Edwards' understanding of the heart of God and his purpose in creation.

Edwards was convinced that the goodness and generosity and grace of God shine forth with greatest brilliance in his commands to you and me. In his sermon "Christian Happiness," he explains: "What could the most merciful being have done more for our encouragement? All that he desires of us is that we would not be miserable, that we would not follow those courses which of themselves would end in misery, and that we would be happy."[2]

Did you hear that? I have to pause for a moment lest that statement slip by unnoticed. Read it again. All that God desires of us is that "we would not be miserable . . . and that we should be happy." Does that sound like the God you've been "serving" these many years? It should. Now let's continue with Edwards as he explains how God goes about fulfilling this great desire. You may find it surprising:

> God, having a great desire to speak after the manner of man, that we should not be miserable but happy, has the mercy and goodness that he forwards us to it, to command us to do those things that will make us so. Should we not think him a prince of extraordinary clemency, he a master of extraordinary goodness, he a father of great tenderness, who never commanded anything of his subjects, his servants, or his children, but what was for their good and advantage? But God is such a king, such a lord, such a father to us.[3]

Every syllable of every statute, every clause of every commandment that ever proceeded from the mouth of God was divinely designed to bring those who would obey into the greatest imaginable happiness of heart. Why? Because God is most glorified in you when you are most satisfied in him![4] Don't swallow God's law like castor oil. For when you understand his intent, it will be like honey on your lips and refreshment to your soul, and duty will appear "sweet and blessed" beyond all comparison.

[2]Jonathan Edwards, "Christian Happiness," in Jonathan Edwards, *Sermons and Discourses 1720–1723*, ed. Wilson H. Kimnach, vol. 10 of The Works of Jonathan Edwards (New Haven, Conn.: Yale University Press, 1992), 304.
[3]Ibid.
[4]See John Piper, *The Pleasures of God* (Portland, Ore.: Multnomah, 1991), 215–216.

APPENDIX
A CHRONOLOGY OF THE LIFE, MINISTRY, AND WRITINGS OF JONATHAN EDWARDS[1]

THE CITATIONS THAT READ "Yale" followed by the volume and page number refer to the Yale University Press edition of Edwards' works.[2] In addition to the major events in Edwards' life, I have placed in brackets other important developments that were indirectly related to him as well as significant dates in secular history that provide a broader framework for Edwards' activity.

[1701 Yale College established in New Haven, Connecticut]

1703 Born October 5, East Windsor, Connecticut

    Edwards had ten sisters (no brothers), all of whom were at least six feet tall! His paternal grandmother was a chronic adulteress who bore another man's child. She was psychotic, often given to fits of perversity, rage, and threats of violence (her sister murdered her own child, and her brother killed another sister with an ax). She eventually deserted her family and was finally divorced by Jonathan's grandfather.

    Edwards receives extensive theological training from his father during his early years and can read Latin by the age of six, Greek and Hebrew by twelve.

---

[1] I wrote the first draft of this chronology in preparation for a course I taught on the life and theology of Jonathan Edwards at Wheaton College. Upon completing the outline I discovered that Kenneth Minkema had produced a similar timeline. I have freely incorporated into my summary much of Ken's research and am grateful for the groundbreaking work that he has done in this regard and in countless other ways to advance our understanding of Edwards. You can find Ken's "Chronology of Edwards' Life and Writings" in *The Princeton Companion to Jonathan Edwards,* ed. Sang Hyun Lee (Princeton, N.J.: Princeton University Press, 2005), xxiii–xxviii.

[2] The Works of Jonathan Edwards (New Haven, Conn.: Yale University Press).

[1706   Benjamin Franklin born]

1710   January 9, his future wife, Sarah Pierpont, is born, New Haven, Connecticut

1712   Experiences spiritual awakening at East Windsor; builds prayer booth in the swamp (though Edwards did not consider himself to have been truly converted at this time)

1716–20   Undergraduate studies

The average age for beginning college was sixteen. He begins his studies in September at Connecticut Collegiate School at Wethersfield. In October he moves to New Haven to study in the newly built Yale College but soon returns to Wethersfield because of disagreement with tutor Samuel Johnson. Upon Johnson's removal, Edwards returns to New Haven in June. During his senior year (winter of 1719–1720), he falls deathly ill with pleurisy. In September he delivers the valedictory address in Latin.

1719–20   Writes "Of Insects"

1720–21   Preaches first formal sermon, "Christian Happiness"

1720–22   M.A. student at Yale

1721   Intense religious experiences (conversion?) begin
(spring [Apr.?])

Edwards' journey into an all-absorbing love affair with the sweetness of God's presence begins with his meditation on one verse of Scripture:

> "The first instance that I remember of that sort of inward, sweet delight in God and divine things, that I have lived much in since, was on reading those words, 1 Tim. 1:17, 'Now unto the king eternal, immortal, invisible, the only wise God, be honor and glory for ever and ever, Amen.' As I read the words, there came into my soul, and was as it were diffused thro' it, a sense of the glory of the Divine Being; a new sense, quite different from any thing I ever experienced before. Never any words of Scripture seemed to me as these words did. I thought with myself, how excellent a being that was; and how happy I should be, if I might enjoy that God, and be rapt up to God in Heaven, and be as it were swallowed up in Him. I kept saying, and as it were singing over these words of Scripture to myself; and went to pray to God that I might enjoy him; and prayed in a manner quite different from what I used to do, with a new sort of affection" (*Personal Narrative*).

1721   Writes "Of the Rainbow," "Of Light Rays"; begins work on "Natu-
              ral Philosophy," "Of Atoms," "Of Being," "Prejudices of the Imagi-
              nation"

1722 (Aug.) Pastors a Presbyterian church in New York City
–1723 (Apr.)

              In late fall of 1722 he begins to record his *Resolutions*. The seven-
              tieth, and last resolution, is written on August 17, 1723. In Decem-
              ber, he starts a spiritual diary in which he writes intermittently from
              1722 to 1725, with four additional entries in 1734–1735. During
              this period he also begins the "Catalogue" of books he had read
              or wished to read. (By the time Edwards arrives in New York, he
              has been embroiled for nearly eighteen months in an argument with
              his father and mother concerning the nature of conversion [Yale
              10:261–278]. Writes in his diary on August 12, 1723: "The chief
              thing, that now makes me in any measure to question my good es-
              tate, is my not having experienced conversion in those particular
              steps wherein the people of New England, and anciently the dissent-
              ers of Old England, used to experience it, wherefore, now resolved,
              never to leave searching till I have satisfyingly found out the very
              bottom and foundation, the real reason, why they used to be con-
              verted in those steps.")

1722 (Sept.) Timothy Cutler, rector of Yale, together with one of the two tutors
              and five local ministers, declare they have converted to Anglicanism
              (this comes to be known as "The Great Apostasy"). Anglicanism is
              feared because of its accommodation to "Arminian impulses" (Yale,
              14:50), its openness to Latitudinarianism, and the potential for cor-
              ruption and authoritarianism in its ecclesiological practices

1722 (Oct.) Writes his first entry in what was to become known as "The Miscel-
              lanies." These entries, of which there are over 1,400, vary in length
              from a short paragraph to several pages:

                   "My method of study, from my first beginning the work of ministry,
                   has been very much by writing; applying myself in this way, to improve
                   every important hint; pursuing the clue to my utmost, when anything
                   in reading, meditation or conversation, has been suggested to my mind,
                   that seemed to promise light in any weighty point. Thus penning what
                   appeared to me my best thoughts, on innumerable subjects for my own
                   benefit. The longer I prosecuted my studies in this method, the more
                   habitual it became, and the more pleasant and profitable I found it"
                   (Letter to the Trustees of the College of New Jersey, Oct. 19, 1757).

1723   Writes "Miscellanies" aa–93

1723 (Apr.) New York City pastorate ends

1723 (May) Returns home to East Windsor

               Writes poem in praise of Sarah Pierpont (she was only thirteen at
               the time)

1723 (Sept.) Receives his M.A. from Yale; his thesis, written in Latin, is on the
               doctrine of imputation (of Adam's sin to his posterity and of Christ's
               righteousness to the believer)

1723 (Sept.) Begins a new notebook titled *The Mind*

1723 (Oct.) Begins *Notes on the Apocalypse*

1723   Writes "Spider Letter"
(Oct. 23)

1723 (Nov.) Writes "Apostrophe to Sarah Pierpont"

1723 (Nov.) Pastors church at Bolton, Connecticut
–1724 (May)

1724   Writes "Miscellanies" 94–146

1724 (Jan.)   Begins *Notes on Scripture*

1724–26   Tutors at Yale (experiences serious illness in the fall of 1725 that
(elected on   lasts three months: "In this sickness God was pleased to visit me
May 21)   again with the sweet influences of his Spirit. My mind was greatly
               engaged there, on divine and pleasant contemplations, and longings
               of soul" [*Personal Narrative*])

               In September of 1724 he has an unidentified spiritual crisis that casts
               him into a depression that lasts for three years. The following entry
               in his diary is dated September 26, 1726:

                    "'Tis just about three years, that I have been for the most part in a
                    low, sunk estate and condition, miserably senseless to what I used to
                    be, about spiritual things. 'Twas three years ago, the week before com-
                    mencement; just about the same time this year, I began to be somewhat
                    as I used to be" (Yale, 16:788).

1725   Writes "Miscellanies" 152–195

1726   Writes "Miscellanies" 196–237, 261–262, 267–274, 313–314

1726   Preaches intermittently at Glastonbury, Connecticut
(Apr.–July)

1726   On August 29 is asked to assist his grandfather, Solomon Stoddard,
            in Northampton; resigns tutorship in September; accepts the call to
            Northampton in November

1727   Writes "Miscellanies" 238–255, 279–305, 315–317

1727   Is ordained on February 15, 1727

1727   Marries Sarah Pierpont
(July 28)

            Experiences a dramatic recovery from the three-year depression (fall
            of 1727).

1727   Massive earthquake shakes New England; a brief spiritual awaken-
(Oct. 29)   ing results. Edwards preaches "Impending Judgments Averted Only
            by Reformation" on December 21, a colony-wide day of fasting

1728   Begins the notebook *Shadows of Divine Things*, later renamed
(Sept. or   *Images of Divine Things*. He continues to add new entries until
Oct.)   1756

1728   First child, Sarah, is born
(Aug. 25)

1728   Writes "Miscellanies" 256–260, 265–266, 275–278, 306–310,
            318–384

1729   Writes "Miscellanies" 385–454

1729   Stoddard dies; Edwards becomes pastor of Northampton church
(Feb. 11)

            The church in 1735 had approximately 620 members. It was cus-
            tomary for Edwards to spend thirteen hours a day in his study.
            However, contrary to widespread opinion, he was anything but an
            academic recluse. He was always available both to his family and his
            congregation and generally received them into his study for counsel-
            ing and prayer.

1729   Edwards experiences "acute emotional and physical fatigue, appar-
(spring)   ently accompanied by a loss of voice, that manifested all the signs
            of an anxiety disorder that modern psychologists often equate with
            creativity" (Yale, 14:13). He takes a seventeen-day trip to New Ha-
            ven (late Apr. to early May), but suffers another collapse in early
            June that makes it impossible for him to preach for a month

[1729 (Dec.) Edwards' sister Jerusha dies of a "malignant fever"]

1730   Writes "Miscellanies" 455–487

1730 (Jan.) Begins "Discourse on the Trinity"

1730   Second child, Jerusha, is born
(Apr. 26)

1730 (Oct.) Makes first entries in his "Blank Bible"

[1731   Edwards may have met Bishop George Berkeley (1685–1753) on a
             trip to Newport]

1731 (Jan.) Writes "Miscellanies" beginning at 488

1731   Purchases "Negro girl named Venus" in Newport, Rhode Island
(May 7)

1731   Preaches "God Glorified in Man's Dependence" at the public lecture
(July 8)   in Boston (based on 1 Corinthians 1:29–31; becomes the first of his
             sermons to be published)

1732   Third child, Esther, is born
(Feb. 13)

1733 (Jan.) Writes "Miscellanies" 612

1733 (Dec.) Writes "Miscellanies" beginning at 625

1734   Fourth child, Mary, is born
(Apr. 7)

1734   Preaches "A Divine and Supernatural Light, Immediately Imparted
(Aug.)   to the Soul by the Spirit of God, Shown to be both a Scriptural, and
             Rational Doctrine"

1734   Preaches series on "Justification by Faith Alone" (Ninety-five pages
(Nov.)   in the Yale edition!); writes "Miscellanies" 668

1734–35   First wave of revival in Northampton and Connecticut Valley occurs

1735   Joseph Hawley, Edwards' uncle, commits suicide by cutting his throat
(June 1)

1734–35   The case of Robert Breck occurs

             First Church, Springfield, decides to call Robert Breck, an Arminian,
             as its pastor. He is installed and ordained in January 1736 despite
             the opposition of a majority of the Hampshire County ministers,
             one of whom is Edwards.

1735   Preaches "The Most High, a Prayer-Hearing God"

1736 (Aug.) Writes "Miscellanies" 698

[1736   Edwards' sister Lucy dies of "throat distemper"]
(Aug. 21)

1736   Fifth child, Lucy, is born
(Aug. 31)

1736   Joseph Bellamy comes to study with Edwards
(fall–winter)

1737   *A Faithful Narrative of Surprising Conversions* published (be-
            tween 1737 and 1739 it went through three editions and twenty
            printings)

            On March 13 the gallery in Edwards' church splits in the middle
            and crashes down on the parishioners below. No one dies. A new
            meetinghouse is dedicated on December 25.

[1738   John Wesley begins Methodist revivals in England]

1738   Preaches "The Excellency of Christ"

1738   Preaches "Charity and Its Fruits" (published in 1851)
(Apr.–Oct.)

1738   Sixth child and first son, Timothy, is born
(July 25)

1738 (Oct.) Writes "Miscellanies" 756

1739 (Feb.) Writes "Miscellanies" 788

1739   Preaches series of thirty sermons on the "History of the Work of
(Mar.–Aug.) Redemption," based on Isaiah 51:8 (published in 1774)

1739 (Aug.) Writes "Miscellanies" 807

1739   Writes "Miscellanies" 832
(winter)

1740 (Jan.) Writes "Miscellanies" 841

1740   Seventh child, Susannah, is born
(June 20)

1740 (Aug.) Writes "Miscellanies" 847

1740   George Whitefield's preaching tour of New England sparks First
            Great Awakening (1740–1742)

Whitefield arrives in Northampton on October 17 and preaches Sunday morning and again in Edwards' home that evening, as well as three more times over the next two days. Whitefield reported that Edwards "wept during the whole time of the exercise." According to Edwards, "the congregation was extraordinarily melted by every sermon; almost the whole assembly being in tears for a great part of sermon time" (Yale, 4:545).

1740 (Nov.) Preaches "They Sing a New Song"; writes "Miscellanies" 859–860

1740 (Dec.) Writes *Personal Narrative*

1741 (May) Writes "Miscellanies" 862

1741   Preaches "Sinners in the Hands of an Angry God"
(July 8)

1741   Writes "Miscellanies" 874; Great Awakening peaks in Northampton
(Aug.–Sept.)

1741   Preaches "Distinguishing Marks of the Work of the Spirit of God"
(Sept. 10) as the Yale commencement speech

1741 (Dec.) Samuel Hopkins arrives at Edwards' home (Hopkins would later become the only eyewitness to write a biography of Edwards). Of Edwards, he said:

> "Though he was of tender constitution, yet few students are capable of a closer or longer application, than he was. He commonly spent thirteen hours, every day, in his study. His usual recreation in summer, was riding on horseback and walking. He would commonly, unless prevented by company, ride two or three miles after dinner to some lonely grove, where he would dismount and walk a while. At such times he generally carried his pen and ink with him, to note any thought that might be suggested, and which promised some light on any important subject. In the winter, he was wont, almost daily, to take an axe, and chop wood, moderately, for the space of half an hour or more."

1741 (Dec.) Writes "Miscellanies" 903

[1742   Revival breaks out in Scotland]

1742   Sarah Edwards has ecstatic experiences (Jan. 19–Feb. 4):

> "His account of his wife's spiritual experience is one of the most striking passages in all he ever wrote, and Sarah's own narrative . . . is an amazing testimony to how much of heaven can be enjoyed upon earth."[3]

---

[3]Iain Murray, *Jonathan Edwards: A New Biography* (Edinburgh: Banner of Truth, 1987), 193.

1742   Northampton covenant (a city-wide renewal)
(Mar. 16)

1742 (June) Writes "Miscellanies" 991

1742 (fall– Writes *Some Thoughts Concerning the Present Revival of Religion*
winter)   *in New England*

1742   Begins sermon series (concluded in 1743) that will eventually be
             published as *Religious Affections*

1743   Eighth child, Eunice, is born
(May 9)

1743   Charles Chauncy publishes his response to Edwards, titled *Season-*
(Sept.)   *able Thoughts on the State of Religion in New England*

             Chauncy's overall assessment of the revival: "For myself, I am
             among those who are clearly in the Opinion, that there never was
             such a *Spirit* of *Superstition* and *Enthusiasm* reigning in the Land
             before. . . . A good Number, I hope, have settled into a truly *Chris-*
             tian temper: Tho' I must add, at the same time, that I am far from
             thinking, that the Appearance, in general, is any other than the effect
             of *enthusiastick Heat*. The goodness that has been so much talked
             of, 'tis plain to me, is nothing more, in general, than a *Commotion*
             in the Passions."

1744   Writes "Miscellanies" 1067–1069

1744   "Young Folks' Bible" (or, the "Bad Books") case begins in March
(Mar.)

1744–49   Writes *Types of the Messiah* ("Miscellany" 1069)

1745   Ninth child and second son, Jonathan, is born
(May 26)

1746   Publishes *A Treatise Concerning Religious Affections*

[1746   College of New Jersey (later named Princeton University) is estab-
             lished]

1747   Tenth child, Elizabeth, is born
(May 6)

1747   David Brainerd visits (May 28) and later dies (Oct. 9)
(May–June)

1747 (Oct.) *An Humble Attempt to promote Explicit Agreement and Visible Union of God's People in Extraordinary Prayer for the Revival of Religion and the Advancement of Christ's Kingdom on Earth* published

1748   Daughter Jerusha dies
(Feb. 14)

[1748   Edwards' uncle, John Stoddard—his greatest benefactor—dies]
(June 19)

1748   Writes "Miscellanies" 1101
(summer)

1749   *An Account of the Life of the Late Reverend David Brainerd* published

1749 (Aug.) Writes *An Humble Inquiry into the Rules of the Word of God, Concerning the Qualifications Requisite to a Complete Standing and Full Communion in the Visible Christian Church*

1750   Eleventh child and third son, Pierpont, is born
(Apr. 8)

1750   Dismissed from Northampton pastorate. Among the reasons most
(June 22)   often cited include: his requests for an increase in salary (to provide for eleven children); his response to the practice of "bundling," in which young people were allowed to spend the night in bed together (though sexual intercourse was forbidden); in another matter, his public reading of a list of people accused of wrongdoing along with those who had merely been witnesses and failing to distinguish between the two; and, perhaps most important, his opposition to Stoddard's doctrine of the Lord's Supper as a "converting ordinance"

1750   Preaches his farewell sermon at Northampton on 2 Corinthians 1:14
(July 2)

            Four days after preaching his farewell sermon he writes to John Erskine: "I am fitted for no other business but study, I should make a poor hand at getting a living by any secular employment. We are in the hands of God, and I bless him, I am not anxious concerning his disposal of us." Edwards actually continues to fill the Northampton pulpit on several occasions from July through November, after his dismissal.

1751 (June) Settles in Stockbridge, Massachusetts, as pastor and missionary to Indians

1751 (Mar.)   Writes "Miscellanies" 1180

1751   Family moves to Stockbridge
(Oct. 18)

[1752   Benjamin Franklin conducts electrical experiment with a kite]

1752   Third daughter, Esther, marries Aaron Burr, president of the College
(June 29)   of New Jersey. Their son, Aaron Burr, Jr., will become vice president
              of the United States

1752   Publishes *Misrepresentations Corrected and Truth Vindicated* (a
(summer)   reply to Solomon Williams on the qualifications necessary for
              communion)

1752 (Aug.)   Writes "Miscellanies" 1200

1752   Preaches "True Grace, Distinguished from the Experience of Devils"
(Sept. 28)

1753   Writes his last will and testament
(Mar. 14)

1753 (Apr.)   Completes the first draft of *Freedom of the Will*

1753   Writes "Miscellanies" beginning with 1227
(winter)

1754   Falls into a serious illness that lasts seven months
(summer)

1754 (Dec.)   Publishes *A Careful and Strict Enquiry into the Modern Prevailing
              Notions of Freedom of the Will*

1755   Reads recently completed *Dissertation on the End for Which God
(Feb. 11–13) Created the World* to Bellamy and Hopkins; finishes *The Nature of
              True Virtue* shortly thereafter (published in 1765)

1755   Timothy Edwards, Jonathan's father, finally ends his ministry in East
              Windsor at the age of eighty-seven

1756   Writes "Miscellanies" beginning with 1281

1757   Writes "Miscellanies" beginning with 1358

1757 (Feb.)   Revival breaks out at the College of New Jersey (Princeton); renews
              Edwards' hopes for genuine outpouring of the Spirit

1757 (May)   Writes final draft of *The Great Christian Doctrine of Original Sin
              Defended*

[1757   Aaron Burr, Edwards' son-in-law and president of the College of
(Sept. 24)   New Jersey, dies]

1757   Trustees of the College of New Jersey write and offer Edwards the
(Sept. 29)   presidency

In his letter of October 19, 1757, Edwards responds to the invitation
of the trustees to take up this new position. Among the reasons why
he feels unfit for the task is the following:

> "I have a constitution in many respects peculiar unhappy, attended with
> flaccid solids, vapid, sizy and scarce fluids, and a low tide of spirits;
> often occasioning a kind of childish weakness and contemptibleness of
> speech, presence, and demeanor; with a disagreeable dullness and stiff-
> ness, much unfitting me for conversation, but more especially for the
> government of a college" (Yale, 16:726).

He also cites what he believes is his deficiency "in some parts of learning, particularly in algebra, and the higher parts of mathematics."

1758   Preaches his farewell sermon to the Indians at Stockbridge
(Jan. 8)

1758   His father, Timothy Edwards, dies
(Jan. 27)

1758   *Original Sin* published

1758   Installed as president of the College of New Jersey (now Princeton
(Feb. 16)   University)

1758   Dies of smallpox inoculation at age fifty-four
(Mar. 22)

One month after assuming his position at Princeton, Edwards is inoc-
ulated for smallpox (Feb. 23). He contracts a fever from which he dies
on March 22. His final words were written to his daughter Lucy:

> "Dear Lucy, it seems to me to be the will of God that I must shortly leave
> you; therefore give my kindest love to my dear wife, and tell her, that the
> uncommon union, which has so long subsisted between us, has been of
> such a nature as I trust is spiritual and therefore will continue forever:
> and I hope she will be supported under so great a trial, and submit
> cheerfully to the will of God. And as to my children, you are now to be
> left fatherless, which I hope will be an inducement to you all to seek a
> Father who will never fail you."

Sarah is herself quite ill when she receives the news by letter. On
April 3, she writes to her daughter Esther:

"What shall I say: A holy and good God has covered us with a dark cloud. O that we may kiss the rod, and lay our hands on our mouths! The Lord has done it. He has made me adore his goodness that we had him so long. But my God lives; and he has my heart. O what a legacy my husband, and your father, has left to us! We are all given to God: and there I am and love to be. Your ever affectionate mother, Sarah Edwards."

1758   Daughter Esther dies (leaving two infants, Sally and Aaron. Aaron
(Apr. 7)   will become vice president of the United States but sadly will not
            become a Christian)

1758   Sarah Edwards dies from dysentery in Philadelphia at age forty-eight
(Oct. 2)

The youngest Edwards child, Betty, dies three years later at the age of fourteen. Of the seven daughters, Eunice lives the longest, dying in 1822 at the age of seventy-nine.

1771   Edwards' mother dies at the age of ninety-eight

After Edwards' death, Samuel Hopkins and Joseph Bellamy take up the task of preparing his manuscripts for publication.

Among the many biographical studies of Edwards, the most helpful (in alphabetical order) include the following:

Gura, Philip. F. *Jonathan Edwards: America's Evangelical*. New York: Hill & Wang, 2005. 284 pp.

Marsden, George M. *Jonathan Edwards: A Life*. New Haven, Conn.: Yale University Press, 2003. 615 pp.

Murray, Iain H. *Jonathan Edwards: A New Biography*. Carlisle, Pa: Banner of Truth, 1987. 503 pp.

Tracy, Patricia J. *Jonathan Edwards, Pastor: Religion and Society in Eighteenth-Century Northampton*. New York: Hill & Wang, 1980. 270 pp.

Winslow, Ola Elizabeth. *Jonathan Edwards: 1703–1758, A Biography*. New York: Octagon, 1973 [1940]. 406 pp.

GENERAL INDEX

SCRIPTURE INDEX